"Packed with heart-warming, faith-building testimonies from the persecuted church, *The Forgotten Manifesto of Jesus* helpfully unpacks Jesus' commissioning words to the Seventy-Two evangelists in Luke 10. This book confirms what I consistently witness in student ministry: the good news of Jesus is unstoppable, and is transforming lives in places that we think are unreachable. Read it and be inspired to be a disciple-maker in the mission field of your life."

Tim Adams, General Secretary, International Fellowship of Evangelical Students (IFES)

Phil Moore has over twenty years of experience leading traditional churches. He has become a chronicler of the disciple-making movements through which the gospel is spreading rapidly across some of the hardest-to-reach areas of Asia, Africa and now of the Western world too. Phil is putting this into practice as a disciple-maker in London, UK, and as one of the leaders of Global Catalytic Ministry's disciple-making mission across Europe. Phil is a graduate of the University of Cambridge and the author of *The Bible in 100 Pages* and the *Straight to the Heart* series of devotional commentaries.

THE FORGOTTEN MANIFESTO OF JESUS

How revival in Iran is spreading
across the world

Phil Moore

INTER-VARSITY PRESS
SPCK Group, Studio 101, The Record Hall, 16–16A Baldwin's Gardens, London
EC1N 7RJ, England
Email: ivp@ivpbooks.com
Website: www.ivpbooks.com

First published 2024

British Library Cataloguing-in-Publication Data
A catalogue record for this book is available from the British Library.

ISBN: 978–1–78974–518–4
eBook ISBN: 978–1–78974–519–1

Set in 10.25/13.75 Minion Pro
Typeset in Great Britain by Fakenham Prepress Solutions, Fakenham, Norfolk NR21 8NL
Printed in Great Britain by Clays Limited, Bungay, Suffolk

Produced on paper from sustainable sources

*Inter-Varsity Press publishes Christian books that are true to the Bible and that
communicate the gospel, develop discipleship and strengthen the Church for its mission in
the world.*

*IVP originated within the Inter-Varsity Fellowship, now the Universities and Colleges
Christian Fellowship, a student movement connecting Christian Unions in universities
and colleges throughout Great Britain, and a member movement of the International
Fellowship of Evangelical Students. Website: www.uccf.org.uk. That historic association
is maintained, and all senior IVP staff and committee members subscribe to the UCCF
Basis of Faith.*

Contents

Contents

Notes to the reader

This book contains brief descriptions of the violent persecution of Christians, including references to sexual violence. Reader discretion advised.

Contact us at: manifesto@catalyticministries.com

Iran: Before the revival

What would you say if we told you that the greatest evangelist of the past fifty years wasn't Billy Graham or Reinhard Bonnke or any other Western preacher? What would you say if we told you that the greatest evangelist of the past century was a hardline Islamic dictator of Iran, named Ayatollah Khomeini? Would you be offended? Would you stop reading this book before you even started? Or would you be curious enough to listen to the story of the God who loves to overcome the forces of darkness where they appear the strongest? We want to share with you how God has chosen to reveal his glory by bringing a great revival to Iran, and by using that revival to spread the good news of Jesus to unlikely people in unlikely places all around the world.

The story begins in downtown Tehran, amid the mosques and the mullahs and the hardened Muslims of Iran. On April 1, 1979, a revolution toppled the Shah of Persia. The ancient Kingdom of Persia became the Islamic Republic of Iran, and Ayatollah Khomeini emerged as its Supreme Leader. One of his first moves was to establish a theocracy: from then on, Iran would be governed by strict Sharia Law. To Christians, this seemed disastrous, but its long-term effect has been to lay bare the true face of Islam. The harsh regime of the ayatollahs has persuaded the nation of Iran, first, that God is real and, second, that he isn't to be found within Islam. It has created an intense hunger for God that cannot be satisfied by empty laws and savage beatings and forcing women to wear headscarves. Against all odds and against all predictions, the Lord has used Ayatollah Khomeini and his friends to turn the hearts of the Iranians toward the gospel of his Son, Jesus Christ.

Here is the big secret that the Iranian government doesn't want you to know: the country's mosques are empty![1] Most people think of Iran as a Muslim nation that wants to export radical Islam to the rest of the world, but Iran's dirty secret is that its Islamic government can't even keep hold of the hearts of its own people. The ruling classes remain religious because that's the way to win the best-paid jobs, but the ordinary people are turning away from the Muslim faith in droves. God has used the rule of the ayatollahs to prepare the people of Iran to receive Jesus as their Savior. I am going to describe for you how God has made Iran his crucible in which to teach a group of persecuted believers how he wants his Church to go about completing his Great Commission.

The Islamic Revolution promised to bring paradise to Iran. Instead, it turned the country into a living nightmare. Ayatollah Khomeini and his successor, Ayatollah Khamenei, who became Supreme Leader in 1989, both claimed to be theocratic leaders – men empowered to hear the words of God and to rule Iran in his name. They promised people heaven, but what they gave them was a taste of hell. Almost a decade of war against Iraq was followed by three decades of economic sanctions from the West. To make matters worse, plain-clothed secret policemen began patrolling the streets to enforce a strict version of Islamic Law. Women whose hair poked out from under their headscarves might expect to be beaten up, or worse. Men who dared to question the regime would be bundled into the backs of cars and never seen again. Iran plunged into economic depression. The supposed Islamic paradise now has more drug addicts per capita than any other nation in the world, as well as the highest divorce

---

1   "Senior Cleric Claims Religion In Iran Weak, 50,000 Mosques Closed," *Iran International:* https://www.iranintl.com/en/202306027255, viewed on May 29, 2024.

2

rate and the highest number of female suicides in the Middle East. Millions of Iranians long to flee to the West, and around 150,000 of them succeed each year.

The first thirty-five years after the Revolution were terrible days to be an Iranian, but they were exciting days to be an Iranian Christian. The Church was still small enough to fly under the radar, so the ayatollahs paid it little attention. The Iranians were devoted in their hearts to God yet falling out of love with Islam, so the Christian message started spreading rapidly across the nation. Believers needed to be careful about how they shared the gospel. They gift-wrapped the Bibles that they gave to people to make them look like harmless presents. They passed around the *Jesus* movie on unmarked SD cards. But as long as they were careful not to rub the noses of the secret police in what they were doing, they were largely left alone. There were a few arrests here and there, but for the most part the Iranian believers look back on that period as a happy harvest time.

Eventually, however, the advance of the Christian gospel across Iran became too obvious for the government to ignore it. In 2014, Ayatollah Khamenei went on television to issue a fatwa against Christianity in general, and against the Iranian house churches in particular. He accused the believers of deceiving young Muslims and of posing a threat to national security. The following day, the secret police took in thousands of church leaders for brutal interrogation.

If you want to gain a flavor of what it was like for the Iranian believers during this wave of fierce persecution, then go onto YouTube and search for *Sheep Among Wolves: Part II.* This is a documentary that was made about the Christians who began the disciple-making movement which today has become known as Global Catalytic Ministries. The video has been watched by millions of people, making it one of the most watched Christian documentaries of all time. It tells the story of a little group of Iranian believers who sought to remain faithful to Jesus in the years after the issuing of this fatwa.

Police interrogations in Iran can be very different from those in the West. They often include beatings, sleep deprivation and other forms of torture. One of the techniques that the secret police may use to extract information is to force men to watch while they rape their wives. The *Sheep Among Wolves* believers debated the godly response to this in one of their underground meetings. After a long discussion among the men, one of their women finally spoke up: "If this happens, I will surrender my body as a living sacrifice, just like it says in Romans 12:1. After all, what are fifteen minutes of rape compared to an eternity with Jesus?" When she said this, all of the men started weeping. If one of their women walked so closely with Jesus that she could say this, then the rest of the believers resolved that they would learn to walk this closely with Jesus too.

Nevertheless, as the weeks turned into months, and the months turned into years, their resolve began to fail. Each time news hit that another of their leaders had been arrested, they would go into a flurry. They would rush to the leader's home to salvage Bibles and to destroy any contact information that might lead the secret police to the other members of their house-church network. Many of their number went into hiding. Others fled to Turkey or the West. Sad to say, a large proportion of their people renounced their faith and dropped out of church life altogether.

For a long time, it felt as though the devil had won the spiritual battle for Iran. The believers featured in the *Sheep Among Wolves* documentary were merely one of many house-church networks, but their experience was representative of Iran as a whole. There were 5,000 believers across their house churches when the fatwa was issued; at the end of three years, only 250 of those believers remained. In all of the different house-church networks across Iran, people felt utterly down-and-out and defeated, as harassed and helpless as sheep among wolves.

And yet, amid the misery that was unleashed by this violent fatwa, the Lord was preparing Iranian hearts to rediscover the Forgotten Manifesto of Jesus and to share its message with the world.

Introduction: The Forgotten Manifesto of Jesus

Over a hundred and fifty years before Ayatollah Khamenei issued his fatwa, a sixteen-year-old schoolboy in England was rediscovering the Forgotten Manifesto of Jesus.

Hudson Taylor would go on to lead one of the greatest disciple-making movements of the nineteenth century, and he explains in his memoirs that it started through his faith in the instructions that Jesus gave to his followers in Luke 10. As he studied those instructions, Hudson Taylor grew convinced that God would grant him gospel breakthrough among the millions of nonbelievers across China if he took Luke 10 as the manifesto for his mission. Although he was still a teenager, he plucked up the courage to tell his church leader that he felt a growing sense that God was calling him to become a missionary to China.

> "How do you propose to go there?" he inquired. I answered that I did not at all know; that it seemed to me probable that I should need to do as the Twelve and the Seventy had done in Judea – go without purse or scrip, relying on Him who had called me to supply all my need. Kindly placing his hand upon my shoulder, the minister replied, "Ah, my boy, as you grow older you will get wiser than that. Such an idea would do very well in the days when Christ Himself was on earth, but not now."

Writing as an old man, Hudson Taylor looks back on his life and reflects on this church leader's reaction to his simple faith in the words of Jesus in Luke 10. "I have grown older since then, but not wiser. I am more than ever convinced that if we were to take the directions of our Master and the assurances He gave to His first disciples more fully as our guide, we should find them to be just as suited to our times as to those in which they were originally given."[2]

This same insight lies at the heart of what the Lord has been doing in recent years in Iran. The Great Commission is of paramount importance to Jesus in all four of the gospels. At the end of Matthew's gospel, he commands his followers to go and make disciples of all nations. At the end of Mark's gospel, he commands them to go into all the world and preach the good news to all creation. At the end of Luke's gospel, Jesus promises to empower his followers to preach forgiveness of sins to every nation in his name. In the final chapters of John's gospel, he spells this out in greater detail. "Very truly I tell you, whoever believes in me will do the works I have been doing, and they will do even greater things than these, because I am going to the Father." "I chose you and appointed you so that you might go and bear fruit – fruit that will last." "As the Father has sent me, I am sending you."[3]

So let me ask you a question. If the Great Commission is so important to Jesus, do you really think he would have left it up to us to figure out how to complete it? Do you think Jesus would have left the Church to muddle its way through 2,000 years of trial and error in order to work out how to make disciples? Of course he wouldn't! In the four gospels, Jesus gives four sets of instructions as to how we are to go about reaching unreached people in his name. He is so confident that these instructions will make us successful in our mission that he doesn't just command us to make a few disciples here and there. He commands us to go and make disciples of all

---

2   Hudson Taylor, *A Retrospect* (originally published 1894; available in multiple editions).

3   Matthew 28:18–20; Mark 16:15–20; Luke 24:45–49; John 14:12, 15:16, 20:21.

nations! That's how confident he is that the instructions he has given us will enable us to make many millions of disciples.

Jesus gives the first set of instructions when he commissions his twelve disciples to take the gospel to the towns and villages of Galilee. His instructions are summarized in Mark 6:7–13 and Luke 9:1–6, and we are given a more complete account in Matthew 10:1–42. Jesus repeats these instructions a few months later, in Luke 10:1–24, when he commissions seventy-two more of his disciples to take the gospel to the remaining towns and villages of Israel. This fourth set of instructions is broadly the same as the three that come before.

Don't miss the significance of this. We tend to talk a lot in our churches about the Great Commission, and rightly so. But all too often, we forget that it is called the Great Commission because two other commissions have come before. The first commission, to the Twelve, is accompanied by fifty-five verses of detailed instruction about how they are to reach Galilee. The second commission, to the Seventy-Two, is accompanied by twenty-four verses of similar instruction about how they are to reach the rest of Israel. The Great Commission comes with very few instructions about how we are to reach the wider world. Jesus simply tells us to "Go and make disciples of all nations, baptizing them in the name of the Father and of the Son and of the Holy Spirit, and *teaching them to obey everything I have commanded you* [my italics]." This is a general command for us to teach our converts to follow all of the instructions of Jesus, but in the context it is also a specific command for us to teach them to follow the instructions for his earlier commissions to the Twelve and the Seventy-Two. Jesus does not feel that he needs to repeat those instructions yet again for his followers to make them the marching manifesto for their mission in every generation.

This is good news for you and me. It means that Jesus cares too much about the fulfilment of his Great Commission to leave us on our own to work out how to go about it. He helped the teenaged Hudson Taylor to birth a movement of disciple-makers across China by following his instructions to the Twelve and to the Seventy-Two. He taught the persecuted Iranian believers to do the same thing when they cried out for him to help them reach their own nation. These instructions lie right at the heart of this *Sheep Among Wolves* story, so before we go any further, please take a moment to read Luke 10 very slowly.

My hope and prayer is that God will equip you to reach your own nation by helping you to rediscover these verses as the Forgotten Manifesto of Jesus.

Luke 10:1–24

[1]After this the Lord appointed seventy-two others and sent them two by two ahead of him to every town and place where he was about to go. [2]He told them, "The harvest is plentiful, but the workers are few. Ask the Lord of the harvest, therefore, to send out workers into his harvest field. [3]Go! I am sending you out like lambs among wolves. [4]Do not take a purse or bag or sandals; and do not greet anyone on the road.

[5]"When you enter a house, first say, 'Peace to this house.' [6]If someone who promotes peace is there, your peace will rest on them; if not, it will return to you. [7]Stay there, eating and drinking whatever they give you, for the worker deserves his wages. Do not move around from house to house.

[8]"When you enter a town and are welcomed, eat what is offered to you. [9]Heal the sick who are there and tell them, 'The kingdom of God has come near to you.' [10]But when you enter a town and are not welcomed, go into its streets and say, [11]'Even the dust of your town we wipe from our feet as a warning to you. Yet be sure of this: The kingdom of God has come near.'

[12]I tell you, it will be more bearable on that day for Sodom than for that town.

[13]"Woe to you, Chorazin! Woe to you, Bethsaida! For if the miracles that were performed in you had been performed in Tyre and Sidon, they would have repented long ago, sitting in sackcloth and ashes. [14]But it will be more bearable for Tyre and Sidon at the judgment than for you. [15]And you, Capernaum, will you be lifted to the heavens? No, you will go down to Hades. [16]Whoever listens to you listens to me; whoever rejects you rejects me; but whoever rejects me rejects him who sent me."

[17]The seventy-two returned with joy and said, "Lord, even the demons submit to us in your name." [18]He replied, "I saw Satan fall like lightning from heaven. [19]I have given you authority to trample on snakes and scorpions and to overcome all the power of the enemy; nothing will harm you. [20]However, do not rejoice that the spirits submit to you, but rejoice that your names are written in heaven."

[21]At that time Jesus, full of joy through the Holy Spirit, said, "I praise you, Father, Lord of heaven and earth, because you have hidden these things from the wise and learned, and revealed them to little children. Yes, Father, for this is what you were pleased to do. [22]All things have been committed to me by my Father. No one knows who the Son is except the Father, and no one knows who the Father is except the Son and those to whom the Son chooses to reveal him."

[23]Then he turned to his disciples and said privately, "Blessed are the eyes that see what you see. [24]For I tell you that many prophets and kings wanted to see what you see but did not see it, and to hear what you hear but did not hear it."

Did you notice that, at the end of these instructions, Jesus describes any eye that can see what he is teaching here as *'blessed'*? That's because not every eye can see it. Unless we humble ourselves to receive God's grace toward us in these verses, we will miss it, like the church leader who laughed at Hudson Taylor for suggesting that these instructions were the Forgotten Manifesto of Jesus for his own day.

And yet that is what these verses truly are. It was when the Iranians rediscovered these verses as the Forgotten Manifesto of Jesus that our *Sheep Among Wolves* story began.

Iran: Go and make disciples

There is a myth that some Christians believe about persecution: that it is exciting, even glamorous, and that it results in rapid church growth. If you could have lived in Iran after the issuing of the fatwa, then you would know this isn't true. Persecution is bewildering and unspeakably painful. For a long time, it didn't look as though any of the Iranian house churches would survive.

One of the Iranian leaders spiraled down into a deep depression. He cried himself to sleep at night and spent his days complaining to the Lord: "Why have you allowed all this to happen? Why have almost all of our believers fled or fallen away? Where are you when we need you?"

He prayed this for three years on the run, before his prayers were finally answered. He heard an audible voice which he sensed in his spirit was the voice of God: "Before the issuing of the fatwa, you were making converts, not disciples. Converts run away in persecution but disciples are willing to die for me. Embrace this crisis as a moment for me to teach you how to make real disciples. Go back out and help people to be taught by my Word and strengthened by my power."

When some of the Iranian leaders gathered to weigh this prophetic word together, they felt deeply convicted of their sin. They felt forced to admit that, during the happy harvest time before the fatwa, they had been so caught up in the large numbers of people who were coming to faith in Jesus that they never stopped to ask themselves whether their gospel impact was as deep as it was wide. They had acted as if the Great Commission were a command to "Go and make converts," but it isn't. It is a command to "Go and make *disciples*." The *Sheep Among Wolves* believers spent considerable time repenting over this together before the Lord.

While they were doing so, they started to hear rumors that "disciple-making movements" were winning millions of people to the Lord in northern India and in several other Asian countries. This seemed to echo the prophetic word they had received, so they decided to find out more. One of their leaders had a foreign passport, so he was able to travel outside Iran to a gathering of the Western missionaries who were mentoring the new disciples in India and elsewhere. When he returned, the Iranian believers gathered together, eager to hear what he had discovered from the missionaries.

He shared that they had challenged him to consider what it truly means for somebody to become a disciple of Jesus. They had asked him to read the story of the thief who was crucified alongside Jesus in Luke 23 and to answer a series of questions.

Did the thief know that Jesus was the Son of God? Well, no, not really.

Did the thief understand the significance of the death and resurrection of Jesus? Not at all.

Did he study the New Testament? No, it hadn't yet been written.

Did he have training in theology? Could he explain the Trinity? No, and no again.

Was he baptized in water? No.

Was he baptized in the Holy Spirit? No.

And yet the thief on the cross had been saved! Becoming a disciple of Jesus is not about a transferal of knowledge, but a transferal of allegiance away from ourselves toward Jesus as our new Master. This is what it means for us to make disciples of Jesus, and it needs to transform how we go about the Great Commission. We need to stop asking ourselves, "How can we persuade people to pray the sinner's prayer with us?" and to start asking instead, "How can we help people to transfer their allegiance away from themselves and onto Jesus as their new Master?"

The missionaries had asked the Iranian leader to open up his Bible at Luke 10 and to read the instructions of Jesus to his early followers. They had taught him to regard this as the Forgotten Manifesto of Jesus, which explains how we are to go into the world and make disciples. It was by following these verses as their missionary manual that they were helping millions of hardened Hindus and Muslims to study stories from the Bible and to come to faith in Jesus. If the persecuted Iranians would humble themselves to learn from what God was teaching their brothers and sisters in other nations, then, the missionaries assured them, they would see similar breakthrough.

We have conducted hundreds of hours of interviews with these Iranian believers. We would love to say that they received this message gladly, but they have been very honest with us that this would not be true. When they first heard that lost people were leading lost people to Jesus in northern India, it made no sense to them. Even if it worked in other nations – and they had their doubts about that – they were certain that it would never work for them across Iran. Iranians have an unhelpful tendency to splinter into sects. That's one of the reasons why they have their own distinct version of Islam. The Shi'ite Muslims of Iran are hated by the Sunni Muslims of the Arab world because they honor twelve imams as saints, worshiping the images of those saints at shrines that the Sunnis despise as hotbeds of idolatry. The Iranian believers were worried that, if they encouraged nonbelievers in their nation to study the Bible together in their homes, they would produce more cults and sects in Iran than there are in America and Europe put together! The idea of allowing the Holy Spirit to speak to people through simple Bible studies sounded to them like heresy. These disciple-making methods might work well in other nations, but they would never work across Iran.

And yet, the Iranian believers felt convicted by a stubborn sense that God was trying to speak to them through these Western missionaries. In spite of their misgivings, they felt the Lord impress upon their spirits that he was trying to answer the questions they had been asking him about how to make disciples. They slowly became convinced that God was calling them to study the instructions of Jesus to the Twelve and to the Seventy-Two, as his Forgotten Manifesto for Iran.

1

Multiply

Luke 10:1

"After this the Lord appointed seventy-two others and sent them two by two ahead of him to every town and place where he was about to go." (Luke 10:1)

Sarah. Rebekah. Rachel. Hannah. Samson's mother. Zechariah and Elizabeth. Reading through the Bible, it is surprising how often God afflicts his followers with barrenness before he enables them to multiply. When the Lord desires to bless his people with patriarchs or with judges or with prophets, he often drives them to their knees in prayer. He causes them to grieve over their infertility and to cry out to him, "Give me children, or I'll die!"

So let me ask you a question. How much does it distress you that the majority of Western Christians fail to produce any spiritual offspring? How shocked are you that most Western churches remain the same size, or shrink smaller, with each passing year? Since Jesus is the Bridegroom and the Church is his Bride, it makes sense that he begins his Forgotten Manifesto by revealing to us how much he longs to help his Bride to multiply. He invites us to face up to our spiritual infertility and to plead with him to entrust us with a growing family.

Each of the three commissions that Jesus gives to his followers in the gospels echoes God's primal command for humanity to multiply. In the very first chapter of the Bible, the Lord commissions Adam and Eve to "Be fruitful and increase in number; fill the earth and subdue it" (Genesis 1:28). Adam and Eve and their descendants have done a pretty good job of this. There are over 8 billion humans on our planet, and people don't have to be clever or well educated or especially gifted to play their part in growing that number. Right across the world, people from every background are having children because God has placed it in our human DNA. In the same way, God has placed it in the DNA of every Christian to multiply disciples. Whenever God gives a command, he empowers us to obey.

"God has placed it in the DNA of every Christian to multiply disciples."

Jesus begins his instructions to his seventy-two disciples in Luke 10 by emphasizing that he wants his followers to multiply. When Jesus sent out the Twelve a few months earlier, he sent them in pairs to proclaim the gospel to the towns and villages of Galilee.[1] He does the same thing for this second mission trip – but with a difference. We are told that "The Lord appointed seventy-two *others* and sent them two by two ahead of him to every town and place where he was about to go [my italics]." This is not a second mission trip for the original Twelve, but for seventy-two *others* from among his wider group of male and female followers.[2]

You don't have to be good at math to spot what is happening here, but let me spell it out for you clearly: seventy-two is six times twelve. For his first mission trip, Jesus sent the Twelve out two-by-two. Now, for this second mission trip, he assigns six new pairs of disciples to each original pair from the Twelve. He begins to train his inner circle of disciples to multiply their ministry to others. Later, he will expect the Seventy-Two to multiply their

---

1 See Mark 6:7. The first mission trip of the Twelve takes place in Matthew 10:1–42; Mark 6:7–13; Luke 9:1–6.

2 We are told about this wider group of disciples in Luke 6:12–17, 8:1–3; Acts 1:15, 1:21–26.

ministry to the 3,000 that he saves on the Day of Pentecost. Twelve becomes Seventy-Two. Seventy-Two becomes thousands. Those thousands become the Church in every nation of the world – right down to your own church today. Jesus wants us to regard such exponential multiplication of disciples as part-and-parcel of normal Christianity. If that isn't our experience, he invites us to cry out to him in prayer.

> ## "Jesus wants us to regard such exponential multiplication of disciples as part-and-parcel of normal Christianity."

In Matthew 28:18–20, when Jesus gives his followers the Great Commission, we are meant to notice that it echoes God's command for Adam and Eve to go forth, increase and multiply. "Go and make disciples of all nations, baptizing them in the name of the Father and of the Son and of the Holy Spirit, and teaching them to obey everything I have commanded you." So let me ask you once again: How shocked do you feel that the churches of the Western world are failing to multiply large numbers of disciples? Do you accept it as normal that the majority of Western Christians are spiritually infertile? The Forgotten Manifesto of Jesus invites us to face up to the fact that something has gone wrong with our churches, and to cry out for God to heal us.

> ## "The Forgotten Manifesto invites us to face up to the fact that something has gone wrong with our churches, and to cry out for God to heal us."

Consider three common reasons why people don't have children. Some are too young to get married; for the time being, at least, they are immature. Others are old enough, but they lack intimacy in their marriage, which is tragic. Others would dearly love to have children, but they are struggling with infertility. In the same way, God invites the Bride of Christ to ask herself: Are we immature? Do we lack true intimacy with Jesus? Is there a problem within our church body which is preventing us from multiplying?

If a mature disciple of Jesus is taught how to walk in daily intimacy with God, they will naturally begin to multiply disciples. They don't have to be special. God has hardwired the ability to multiply into their spiritual DNA. Nothing but *sinfulness* (akin to the immaturity of a child) or *lack of fellowship with the Lord* (akin to estrangement within a marriage) can prevent a Christian from multiplying disciples. Therefore, if we find ourselves struggling to lead the people around us to faith in Jesus, the Forgotten Manifesto begins by inviting us to confess it and to plead with God to help us. If God was willing to heal the wives of Abraham and Isaac and Jacob and Elkanah of their infertility, then how much more can we trust his willingness to heal the Bride of Christ of her spiritual infertility?

The reason why many churches are not multiplying rapidly is not that there is anything wrong with the gospel. The good news of Jesus Christ is still as powerful to save people today as it was when Jesus sent out the Twelve and the Seventy-Two. The Forgotten Manifesto of Jesus calls us back to the belief that a healthy Bride of Christ will always multiply disciples. If this isn't our own experience in our churches, then it invites us to bring this problem to him, honestly and repentantly, on our knees.

India: David's story

My name is David, and I am one of the Western missionaries who trained the Iranian believers when they sent one of their leaders to ask us to help them. I was able to answer their questions because, twenty-five years earlier, I had passed through a similar spiritual crisis of my own.

My wife and I are Americans, but we served as missionaries to the Bhojpuri people of northern India. You may never have heard of them, but they are the twelfth-largest people group on earth. There are over a hundred million Bhojpuri living in the heartland of Hinduism. Varanasi, the holy city of Hinduism, is a majority-Bhojpuri city. After over a hundred and fifty years of Christian missionary endeavor among them, there were barely 5,000 Bhojpuri believers. Everybody warned us that their region had earned the title of "the graveyard of modern mission."

Of course, I thought that I knew better. I had a degree in theology, and I was overflowing with ideas of how we could reach the Bhojpuri with the gospel. I quickly trained up some of the existing believers in the missionary methods I had learned at Bible college. We went out together on evangelistic missions, and we sought to establish a church building in every city. I felt so excited about the breakthroughs that we were about to see together – but instead, I saw the murder of six of our brave evangelists. My life was spared, but the Indian government expelled me from the country. I escaped with my wife and children, with my dreams for the Bhojpuri in tatters.

For many weeks, I sat in the office of my new home in Singapore and wept like I had never wept before. I closed the blinds and just sat there, depressed in the darkness. I have since discovered that this is a valley that many people need to pass through as part of their journey toward stewarding a disciple-making movement. It is only when we "hit the wall" and realize that our own methods can never bring about a mighty move of God that we become ready to embrace what only God can do. Day after day, I cried out to the Lord: "God, I can't plant churches anymore. I didn't sign up to love people, to train people, to send people out, and then to see those people killed. You have to teach me your way to make disciples and plant churches, because I refuse to believe that you would call me to this task without telling me how to accomplish it. Show me in your Word how you want me to reach these people. How am I to make disciples and plant churches among the Bhojpuri?"

During those two months of prayer, I made a radical decision. I resolved not to watch any TV or to read any book other than the Bible until the Lord gave me an answer. I would spend the time I saved reading the Bible from cover to cover. When I finished it, I went back and read it again and again and again. I kept on crying out for God to teach me how to make disciples among the Bhojpuri people – and then one day I suddenly felt a clarity that I knew was from the Lord. It was December 8, 1991, and I had been praying and fasting for so long that my wife and children were worried that something was wrong with me. There wasn't – I was just hungry for God to show me how to make disciples! As I felt the Holy Spirit give me sudden clarity through the Scriptures I had been reading, I started scribbling frantically on the blank back pages of my Bible. What I wrote down was the Discovery Bible Study method that I have been using, unchanged, for the past thirty years.

In that moment of clarity, the Holy Spirit showed me that Luke 10:1–24 was the Forgotten Manifesto of Jesus. Instead of training the Bhojpuri believers in the Western church methods which had gotten six of them killed, I was to return and teach them how

Jesus instructs them to take the gospel to the Bhojpuri people. I began praying for five Bhojpuri men that I could mentor in how to follow this Forgotten Manifesto, then I boarded a plane and trusted God to lead me to them.

One of the first things that I did on my arrival back in northern India was to attend a secret forum on how to evangelize Hindus. I was anxious to know whether the Lord was giving similar insights to other missionaries, but for some reason, known only to God, the main speaker didn't show up. Since the event organizers had gathered 300 people for a three-day forum which was now lacking a main speaker, they panicked and asked if I was willing to speak instead! I embraced it as my God-given opportunity to shout from the rooftops what he had been whispering into my ear in the darkness of my office back in Singapore. I explained to the delegates that Luke 10 is the Forgotten Manifesto of Jesus, and that he is calling us to give up our old missionary methods in order to take nonbelievers on a journey of discovery instead. People listened until I said we mustn't speak the name of Jesus to people too early. Then many of them got agitated. When I shared my vision for nonbelievers leading other nonbelievers to faith in Jesus through Discovery Bible Studies in their homes, some of them stood up and shouted me down as a heretic. By the start of the second day, two-thirds of the forum delegates had left and gone home. When I confessed at the end of the second day that I hadn't yet seen this in action – I was simply sharing by faith what I believed the Lord had shown me in the Bible – the remaining third decided to go home too. By the end of the final day there were only two people left – a Bhojpuri pastor named Victor and another man who was relying on Victor for his lift home! It wasn't a very promising start to our Bhojpuri breakthrough!

But Victor was the first of the five men I had been praying for. The Lord led us both to four more – or, strictly speaking, to three more Bhojpuri men and to one Bhojpuri woman. For a long time, we just studied the Scriptures and prayed together. We saw no churches planted in year one. We saw no churches planted in year two. My missions agency threatened to fire me for my unfruitfulness. Yet as the six of us experimented together to find out what it looked like for us to live out Luke 10 among the Bhojpuri, we slowly began to build momentum. In year three, we planted eight churches together. In year four, we planted forty-eight more. In years five, six and seven, we planted 148, 327 and 527 churches. By the end of year nine, we totaled over 2,000 churches, gathering over 55,000 Bhojpuri believers. Within fifteen years, we had over 80,000 churches and over 2,000,000 Bhojpuri believers – all of this among a people group which had only had 5,000 believers fifteen years before. This is what happens when we ditch our own methods and embrace those of Jesus!

It wasn't as easy as it sounds. When Victor looks back on those fifteen years, there are tears in his eyes: "Doing something totally outside the Christian box was hard. I lost all my friends, I felt very alone and not much was happening on the ground. Many people thought I was crazy because I couldn't explain what I was doing. I had no support, so I leant on God. It was during this time that he revealed himself as my Friend and not just my Creator and Savior. If I hadn't met God in this way, then the movement probably wouldn't have happened. I died to myself, so it became his movement, not my own. If you want to see God do something similar where you are, then my advice is become God's friend. There is nothing more you need to do other than learn to follow him."

By the time I was introduced to the Iranian believers, I had handed over the work among the Bhojpuri to Victor and the other local believers. As missionaries, we aim not to stay anywhere too long. Local leaders learn in the presence of experienced leaders, but they only emerge when those experienced leaders leave. You have to create a leadership vacuum. That's why I have spent the last two decades training up leaders in over ninety-five countries – and then quickly moving on.

People usually tell me that disciple-making movements won't work where they are. But I have seen them happen anywhere that people are humble enough to embrace the Forgotten Manifesto of Jesus.

2

On your knees

Luke 10:2

"He told them, 'The harvest is plentiful, but the workers are few. Ask the Lord of the harvest, therefore, to send out workers into his harvest field.'" (Luke 10:2)

Jesus tells his followers that partnering with him should feel easy: "My yoke is easy and my burden is light" (Matthew 11:30). That's one of the clues God gives us that we need to learn a new model of ministry. He uses our unfruitfulness to alert us to the fact that we need to go back to the instructions of Jesus to his followers in Luke 10. Our *Sheep Among Wolves* story isn't really about India or Iran. It is about rediscovering the words of Jesus.

Too many church leaders are worn-out and weary. They have been told to jump through so many hoops to become successful pastors that the life-giving ministry Jesus has entrusted to them instead feels soul-destroying. So let me ask you a simple question: If pastoring a few hundred believers feels exhausting, how can we ever hope to reach the lost millions through our existing models of ministry? It simply isn't going to happen. The Forgotten Manifesto of Jesus is good news because it lifts the pressure off our shoulders. It teaches us to wear the Great Commission as an easy yoke and a light burden.

Jesus begins by assuring his followers in Luke 10:2 that "the harvest is plentiful." The problem isn't with the harvest fields. It is that "the workers are few." How can you reach a hundred million Bhojpuri with just five leaders? The answer is: you can't. You have to find out where God is at work in the hearts of Bhojpuri nonbelievers so that you can mobilize many of them as co-workers in your mission. In Luke 10:6, Jesus describes such reinforcements from the harvest fields as *People of Peace*. Since he is "the Lord of the harvest," not just the Lord of the Church, we can expect him to be at work in the hearts of unsaved people, drawing them onto our team. Our task is to pray that he will help us to find them and to enlist them as our fellow workers. That's how David and Victor were able to reach 2 million Bhojpuri in fifteen years, and it is how God wants to help us to reach the millions of nonbelievers in our own nations. The Lord is preparing many people's hearts to follow him, and he wants us to pray that he will lead us to them by his Holy Spirit.

That's why the first command of Jesus in his Forgotten Manifesto is for us to pray. His commission to the Twelve began with a call to prayer: "The harvest is plentiful but the workers are few. Ask the Lord of the harvest, therefore, to send out workers into his harvest field" (Matthew 9:37–38). He repeats this as he commissions the Seventy-Two. Disciple-making movements are like sailing ships. Unless we set our sails to catch the wind of God's Spirit, any move of God will pass us by, yet setting our sails right can make no difference until the wind of God's Spirit actually blows! Our faith is not in methods, because methods achieve nothing on their own. Disciple-making movements are all about partnering with God's Spirit, so they always begin with a call to prayer.

> **"Disciple-making movements are all about partnering with God's Spirit, so they always begin with a call to prayer."**

Jesus set the pattern for us. He began his public ministry by spending forty days and nights in prayer and fasting. He did this because he knew that he would fail in his mission if he attempted it by human strength alone. He could only reach the Jewish nation if his Father prepared the hearts of many Jews to become his co-workers and then led him to them by his Holy Spirit. Jesus continued to spend large amounts of his time in prayer, explaining to the crowds that "Very truly I tell you, the Son can do nothing by himself; he can do only what he sees his Father doing, because whatever the Father does the Son also does. For the Father loves the Son and shows him all he does ... By myself I can do nothing."[1] At the start of Luke 10, Jesus is therefore commissioning the Seventy-Two to follow his lead. There are far too many lost people for us to imagine we can reach them on our own. We need to ask the Lord to create co-workers for us within the harvest fields and then to lead us to them.

The early Christians did this. It was one of the reasons why they saw such rapid gospel breakthrough. Instead of rushing prematurely to proclaim the resurrection and ascension of Jesus to the people of Jerusalem, they devoted themselves to ten days of fervent prayer. As a result, when they finally went out into the streets of their city, they found that God had prepared the hearts of 3,000 people to receive their message. Those 3,000 new converts became their co-workers. Instead of weighing the Church down with their problems, they went and shared the gospel with their families and their friends. As a result, "The Lord added to their number daily those who were being saved."[2]

This remained the model for the early church in its mission. We are told that it was "while they were worshiping the Lord and fasting" that the Holy Spirit told them the time had come for the gospel to be taken to the Roman world. Their immediate reaction to this was not to debate strategies or to take up a financial offering. It was to pray for Paul and Barnabas. "After they had fasted and prayed, they placed their hands on them and sent them off."[3]

---

1   John 5:19–20, 5:30. This explains verses such as Luke 4:42, 5:16, 6:12, 9:18, 11:1.

2   Acts 1:13–14, 2:41–47. They remain devoted to prayer in Acts 3:1, 4:24–31, 6:4, 9:11, 10:9, 12:5, 12:12.

3   Acts 13:1–3. This commitment to fervent prayer is echoed in Acts 14:23, 16:16, 16:25. Is it any wonder that the early Christians found so many People of Peace in each city on their travels?

Prayer is primarily about partnership with God. Although he rules in heaven, we are told in Psalm 115:16 that God has firmly resolved to rule on earth through the prayers of his people. Although he could complete the Great Commission in a single day through his mighty army of millions of angels, he has decided to complete it more slowly through you and me so that he can use the process to help us forge a deeper friendship with him. Prayer is how we get to discover what God is doing in the world and how we learn to partner with him in his harvest of humanity. As *Sheep Among Wolves*, we have learned that there are seven essential elements toward seeing a movement of disciple-makers reach a nation. We have listed these "7 Es" for you below (see Figure 2.1) but, before you read them, please grasp that this is not mere methodology. We do not place our hope for gospel breakthrough in these seven elements, vital though they are. We place our hope in the Lord of the harvest, recognizing that we can only achieve each of these elements through fervent prayer.

First, we pray for God to make us disciples of Jesus who are worthy of the name. This is essential to our mission. Why would we expect our lives to attract anyone to Jesus if we are living part-for-Jesus and part-for-the-world? Fish multiply fish. Birds multiply birds. Animals multiply animals after their own kind. In the same way, half-hearted Christians reproduce more half-hearted Christians like themselves. God knows that the world already has enough of those! He wants us to become disciples worth multiplying, and this can only happen as we develop a holy friendship with him through a life of fervent prayer.

Second, we pray that God's kingdom will come all around us, since the Bible informs us that there is a fierce spiritual battle raging in the heavenlies for the world. Jesus has asked his Father to give him every nation, but demons do not give up territory lightly that has been theirs uncontested for many years. That's why prayer movements tend to precede disciple-making

29

Element #1
Be a real disciple to make disciples

Element #2
Pray and mobilize prayer

Element #3
Engage tribes of lost people

Element #4
Find the People of Peace

Element #5
Help them to start Discovery Groups

Element #6
Help them to transition into Multiplying House Churches

Element #7
Coach emerging leaders to go and reach further

Figure 2.1 The "7 Es" – seven essential elements for disciple-making

movements. We must mobilize an army to fight alongside the angels in prayer to dislodge the enemy. We do not need to pray *for* victory, since Jesus has already defeated the devil and his demons, but we do need to pray *from* victory, mobilizing the prayers of many to evict demonic squatters from ground they have no right to own.

> **"We do not need to pray *for* victory, since Jesus has already defeated the devil and his demons, but we do need to pray *from* victory."**

We have found that fasting is a mighty accompaniment to our prayers. We don't fast to move the heart of God, since he already desires to give us gospel breakthrough. We fast to move the principalities and powers that stand against us. Demons possess real authority on earth through human sin, but when we fast we declare that we no longer belong to this present sinful age. We are people who hunger for heaven as our true home and who will not rest until God gives the nations to Jesus as his inheritance.

In the book of Daniel, when the prophet discovers that the Lord has promised to restore the land of Israel to the Jewish people, he begins a three-week fast to dislodge the demons that are resisting the fulfilment of God's promises. "I ate no choice food; no meat or wine touched my lips; and I used no lotions at all until the three weeks were over." After twenty-one days, Daniel receives a visit from an angel who informs him that "Since the first day that you set your mind to gain understanding and to humble yourself before God, your words were heard … but the prince of the Persian kingdom resisted me twenty-one days." Note what this teaches us. The Lord is so committed to ruling the earth through his people that he permits demons to resist his purposes until he finds human partners who will pray and fast for breakthrough. Daniel says about God's angel: "I took my stand to support and protect him." That's a pretty amazing thing for us to be able to say about partnering with God![4]

Jesus addresses the other five elements of the "7 Es" in his instructions to the Seventy-Two. In telling them to pray for People of Peace to emerge as their co-workers from the harvest fields, he is warning them that reaching the world with the gospel isn't something we can ever do for God. We cannot pay God back for saving us by leading other people to him. Our gospel fruitfulness makes us even more indebted to him: not only has he graciously saved us, but now he graciously allows us to partner with him too. Only God can enable us to engage successfully with new groups of lost people. Only God can help us to identify correctly which of them are People of Peace. Only God can empower us to help them start Discovery Groups which will go on to become Multiplying House Churches. Only God can enable us to coach and release emerging leaders from those churches to travel to other places in order to carry on their disciple-making movement elsewhere.

The Great Commission is impossible, from start to finish. It was always meant to be. Hoping to birth a movement of disciple-makers without prayer is like hoping to travel to the moon without a rocket. Jesus assures us that it simply can't be done.

> **"Hoping to birth a movement of disciple-makers without prayer is like hoping to travel to the moon without a rocket."**

When Hudson Taylor looked back on birthing a movement of disciple-makers in China, he reflected that "It is always helpful to fix our attention on the Godward aspect of Christian work; to

---

4 Daniel 10:2–3, 10:13, 11:1. When Daniel grasps God's plan to save his nation, he doesn't treat it as a done deal. "I, Daniel, understood from the Scriptures ... so I turned to the Lord *God and pleaded with him in prayer and petition, in fasting, and in sackcloth and ashes*" (Daniel 9:2–3, my italics). We get to do the same thing for our own nations today.

realize that the work of God does not mean so much man's work for God, as God's own work through man … The great need, therefore, of every Christian worker is to know God."[5]

God has firmly decided not to save the world without us. Without him, we cannot; yet without us, he will not. That's why Jesus begins his Forgotten Manifesto by commanding us to pray: "Ask the Lord of the harvest, therefore, to send out workers into his harvest field."

---

5 Hudson Taylor, *A Retrospect* (1894).

Iran: Early days of revival

It took the Iranian believers some time to accept what David and the other Western missionaries were trying to teach them. Some of them had been believers for many years, so they thought they already knew their Bibles. The idea of holding back on preaching Jesus in order to take skeptics on a journey of discovery sounded wrong to them. Nor did it make any sense to them that the Lord might be preparing People of Peace for them within the harvest fields of Iran. How could nonbelievers be of any help to the house churches in leading other nonbelievers to faith in Jesus?

Looking back, the Iranians freely confess that their doubts were driven by pride. In the days before the fatwa, they had led thousands of people to faith in Jesus, so they felt that they were experts on the Great Commission. Western missionaries ought to be learning from them, not the other way around! Their past successes might have robbed them of the future God had for them.

But by God's grace, they found themselves in a position where they had no real choice but to listen. There was no way they could persist in preaching the name of Jesus openly, since they would be arrested. They had to learn how to take people on a journey of discovery instead. Nor did they have any real alternative to seeking out People of Peace within the harvest fields of Iran. There were 85 million Iranians, most of whom were under thirty, so there was no way that the tiny remnant of believers could ever hope to reach so many millions on their own. They had no option but to try out David's teaching about the Forgotten Manifesto of Jesus. They began pleading with the Lord of the harvest to mobilize Iranian nonbelievers to help them re-evangelize their nation.

It took them five years to see the first signs of breakthrough. Five long years! They nearly gave up so many times. They had to keep asking themselves: Are we going to believe what our eyes tell us or what God's Word promises us? Who wants to see our nation saved more – us or Jesus? This experience of delay is common to the many other nations where movements of disciple-makers are growing exponentially. Whenever Christians embrace the Forgotten Manifesto of Jesus, it seems to take two to three years on average to gain traction. Maybe that's how long it takes for God to deal with our stubborn pride and sinfulness, or how long it takes us to unlearn our old ways of ministering and learn the essentials of disciple-making movements instead. Whatever the reason, it shouldn't surprise us. If it took Jesus three years before he could release the Twelve and the Seventy-Two into the Great Commission, then it is likely to take us some time too.

Maybe it took five years of prayer for the Iranians to assert their spiritual victory in the heavenlies. The Bible tells us that every promise of God to us is yes and amen in Jesus, but it also warns us that principalities and powers still stand against us. Demons that have held onto territory for decades, even for centuries, cannot be expected to relinquish that territory without a fight. During those five years, the Iranians learned how to pray aggressively, not just asking God to bless their nation but asserting the victory of Jesus over the devil. There is a world of difference between asking God to bless us and declaring to demons that they must surrender territory to us in Jesus' name.

The Iranians drew inspiration from the prophet Daniel, who pleaded with God for the salvation of God's people during the days of the Persian Empire. In Daniel 10:2–3, we are told that Daniel fasted from all but the most basic of foods in order to partner with the Lord in prayer: "I ate no choice food; no meat or wine touched my lips; and I used no lotions at all until the three weeks were over." Since this is how Daniel drove back demons to secure revival for his people, the Iranians began fasting from meat, salt, oil, sugar, bread, rice and pasta. They ate nothing except for fruit, vegetables, lentils and nuts for three weeks at a time. They were not fasting for the sake of fasting. Daniel had a specific goal in mind and so did they. They wanted to see happen in Iran what David and his friends had seen happen among the Bhojpuri. They were desperate for God to lead them to the People of Peace that he was preparing to become their co-workers. One of the things about a "Daniel fast" is that you never feel hungry, since you can eat as often as you like, but you feel perpetually dissatisfied. This can be a powerful stimulus to persistent prayer. Every time the Iranians felt dissatisfied in their stomachs, they asked God to satisfy their craving to see the victory of Jesus in the heavenlies.

Another Bible passage that inspired the Iranians was in the book of Esther, where the people of God were saved from being persecuted by the Persians. We are told in Esther 4:15–16 that she and her friends fasted completely from food and water for three days and nights. This was a desperate measure fueled by desperate need, and the Lord answered Esther's prayer. The Iranians therefore started to intersperse their three-week "Daniel fasts" with three-day nil-by-mouth "Esther fasts."

Many of the believers dropped out of the house churches during this long season of intense prayer and fasting. They didn't fall away from the Christian faith. They simply left to join other groups of believers who were pursuing more traditional methods of ministry. Meanwhile, the believers who remained developed a deeper relationship with God. They came to see that ministry *to* God must precede ministry *for* God. As they spent time studying the Scriptures together, seeking to understand how Jesus wanted them to make disciples, they discovered that waiting on God in prayer and worship is one of the most productive things we can ever do to serve him.

During those five years, the Iranian believers experimented with the ways that David and the other Western missionaries were teaching them to share the gospel with people. At first, the successes were few and far between. But as they confessed that they had sinned against the Lord by attempting to start something for him instead of asking him to open their eyes to what he was doing all around them, they began to see the first signs of breakthrough.[6] As they began praying less and less for the persecution to end and more and more for God to lead them to the People of Peace he was preparing in the Iranian harvest fields, something seemed to shift for them. The things that they had heard about among the Bhojpuri began to happen in their own nation too.

God began to surprise the Iranians by leading them to many People of Peace, even in the midst of continued persecution. By now, they had learned not to scare them off by being over-eager, but instead to help them take their family and friends on a journey of discovery. Since Persian culture is extremely hospitable, each of these People of Peace was able to spread the gospel through their entire family and social network. Soon the 250 believers in the *Sheep Among Wolves* network of house churches had become a thousand. The thousand very quickly became several thousand. The fatwa had not been lifted, but a sense of defeat had been lifted away. A new season of happy harvest time had begun again across Iran – only this time, the believers were no longer making converts. They were making real disciples who obeyed the Lord in everything.

---

6 We have come to view this as a modern form of Sabbath-breaking. Disciple-making movements are all about discovering the work that God has been doing in people's hearts ahead of us. See Deuteronomy 6:10–12.

3

Weakness is our superweapon

Luke 10:3

"Go! I am sending you out like lambs among wolves." (Luke 10:3)

When would you say the Church started? Would you date it back to the moment when the Holy Spirit descended on the 120 believers on the Day of Pentecost? Take a moment to reflect on what that would mean. It would make the four gospels a mere warm-up act to church history – an account of how there came to be a group of believers to start the Church, but not an account of how we are to go out and start new churches ourselves. Such a view would be at odds with the apostle Paul, since he urges us to "Follow my example, as I follow the example of Christ" (1 Corinthians 11:1).

What Paul and the other writers of the New Testament want us to grasp is that the Church didn't start when the Holy Spirit fell at Pentecost. It started when the Holy Spirit descended on Jesus at his baptism in the Jordan River. This simple insight is revolutionary. It teaches us to read the four gospels with new eyes, as an account of Jesus starting the first church, then calling us to multiply it by following his lead. In everything he did, he sought to teach his first group of followers how to follow his Forgotten Manifesto.

When we read the gospels afresh in this way, one of the first things that strikes us is how determined Jesus was to start his Church through "little people." A few of the people he called to follow him were learned teachers, such as Nicodemus and Joseph of Arimathea, but for the most part Jesus started his Church through

38

weak and ordinary men and women. His enemies dismissed his followers as "sinners," as "unschooled, ordinary men" and as ignorant "Galileans," because none of them looked remotely strong enough to steward a disciple-making movement that would spread to every corner of the world.[1]

In a moment, when you meet some of the Iranian house-church leaders, you will discover that our *Sheep Among Wolves* story is a tale of "little people." When church leaders from the West visit Iran, they usually expect to find an elite special-forces team of Christians. They are astonished to discover that God is using people to lead churches who would scarcely be permitted to put out the chairs in their own churches back home. Many of them are former drug dealers and prostitutes and Islamic hardliners. They are people from the bottom end of society, whose lives have been so transformed by the power of God that they cannot keep the good news to themselves. The more messed up a person is, the more the Lord seems to delight in using them to lead the ranks of his growing gospel army.

That's why we ought to feel encouraged that the Forgotten Manifesto of Jesus continues: "Go! I am sending you out like lambs among wolves." This might seem like a strange encouragement, since lambs get eaten by wolves, but what Jesus is teaching us here is that he is such a strong Shepherd that he can afford to partner with the weakest sheep. We were happy for the documentary that was made about these Iranian believers to be entitled *Sheep Among Wolves*, because we want to prove to the world that Jesus delights to build his Church through "little people." This isn't about marketing our ministry. It's about the posture that we have learned to take in obedience to the words of Jesus in Luke 10. The weaker and more vulnerable we feel, the more of the glory goes to him![2]

---

1   Matthew 9:9–13, 11:19; Mark 2:14–17; Luke 5:27–32, 7:34–50, 19:7; Acts 2:7, 4:13.

2   Jesus also says this to the Twelve in Matthew 10:16–25. It is part-and-parcel of obedience to Jesus.

"The weaker and more vulnerable we feel, the more of the glory goes to him!"

For this reason, we have come to regard weakness as our superweapon. If we were stronger, God might hesitate to use us, since we might attribute our successes to ourselves. Jesus makes it clear that he isn't looking for the best and brightest workers. He came to save the sick and not the healthy. He ascended back to heaven to empower the weak and not the strong. The apostle Paul encourages us to celebrate this:

> Think of what you were when you were called. Not many of you were wise by human standards; not many were influential; not many were of noble birth. But God chose the foolish things of the world to shame the wise; God chose the weak things of the world to shame the strong. God chose the lowly things of this world and the despised things – and the things that are not – to nullify the things that are, so that no one may boast before him. (1 Corinthians 1:26–29)

If this is true, then it doesn't matter if the People of Peace we find in the harvest fields seem rather ordinary and unimpressive. Jesus loves to do great things through "little people," so that all the glory goes to him.

What the Iranian believers lacked in talent they more than made up for in obedience. They were so grateful to the Lord for saving them out of their darkness that they offered no half-measures in their devotion to him. Very quickly, their disciple-making movement spread over the border into Afghanistan. There are few places on earth where Christians feel more like sheep among wolves than in the nation that is governed by the Taliban. Yet even in Afghanistan, they discovered that the Lord led them to many People of Peace whose hearts he had been preparing to receive the good news about Jesus.

One of the major features of disciple-making movements is an emphasis on radical, immediate obedience to God as he speaks to us by his Spirit through his Word. It isn't for leaders to tell people what to do, since that can easily become abusive, but it is for each believer to discern what God is saying to them and to surrender their heart to him totally. Jesus tells us that obedience is the believer's "love language" toward God. "Anyone who loves me will obey my teaching … Anyone who does not love me will not obey my teaching."[3] Obedience is therefore not about rules, but about our relationship with God as our Father.

"Jesus tells us that obedience is the believer's 'love language' toward God."

Most of us instinctively worship *comfort* and *convenience* and being in *control*. One of the reasons why "little people" often make the best disciples is that they never have these three things to begin with! They have much less to lose by embracing *discomfort*, *inconvenience* and loss of *control* in order to let Jesus live out his life through them by his Holy Spirit. The Iranian believers began to see breakthrough by regarding "little people" as potential leaders of a hundred or a thousand. Instead of looking at people on the outside, based on how much they had left to learn about following Jesus, they learned to look on the inside, at how much the hand of God was at work within them. They were happy to be labeled *Sheep Among Wolves*, because they knew that God loves to reveal his power through "little people," to ensure that all the glory for gospel fruitfulness goes entirely to him.

This is what enables disciple-making movements to keep on growing, rather than collapsing under the weight of their successes. The bar is kept low enough for leaders to multiply rapidly, so that the

---

3   John 14:15, 14:21, 14:23–24, 15:10.

burden of discipling new believers never falls on too few shoulders. Instead of getting worn out by growth, the longtime Christians feel invigorated in their faith by seeing nonbelievers rise up quickly to play their part in the Church's mission. They feel like the Christians in the book of Acts – so excited by what they see God doing in the lives of those around them that they gladly give up everything to partner with him. Could it be that many churches around the world are stalling in their mission because they have not learned how to release "little people" to lead as "lambs among wolves"?

The Lord longs to save the people of every nation, not just people in Iran and Afghanistan. So let's embrace what the Forgotten Manifesto of Jesus tells us here:

God loves to do great things through "little people."

4

Stripped down to size

Luke 10:4

"Do not take a purse or bag or sandals." (Luke 10:4)

What if you don't see yourself as a "little person"? What if you live in a part of the world where the fatal lure of *comfort, convenience* and *control* feels very strong? Well, don't worry. God has a way of stripping down to size the cleverest and the strongest people so that he can use them. Jesus addresses this when he commands his followers in his Forgotten Manifesto: "Do not take a purse or bag or sandals."

Most of us believe, deep down, that our problems in partnering with God stem from the fact that we are too weak for him to use us. However, the story of Gideon in the book of Judges insists that our problem is actually that we fool ourselves that we are strong. Gideon is preparing to fight an army that has invaded Israel when, for the first time in the Bible, the Lord confesses that he is unable to do something. "You have too many men. I cannot deliver Midian into their hands, or Israel would boast against me, 'My own strength has saved me'" (Judges 7:2). It is only after God has whittled down the strength of Gideon's army from 32,000 soldiers to a mere 300 that he finally feels able to entrust Gideon with victory. Before that, he knew that Gideon would be tempted to steal some of the credit for his victory. It is only by stripping Gideon down to size that the Lord feels ready to use him. Are you willing for the Lord to strip you down to size too?

This is what Jesus seeks to do for us in his Forgotten Manifesto. He tells the Seventy-Two that their problem isn't that they are less gifted than his inner group of Twelve. It is that they may be tempted to think that they have certain skills which qualify them to play a part in God's great mission. Finding People of Peace isn't difficult – it is impossible – so human strength is a hindrance rather than an advantage. They will only find co-workers in the harvest fields if they allow the Lord to strip them of their purses and their moneybags, even their spare set of shoes. In order to draw down heavenly resources, we need to throw away any earthly resources on which we might be tempted to rely.[1]

> **"Finding People of Peace isn't difficult – it is impossible – so human strength is a hindrance rather than an advantage."**

Perhaps this is why the Lord decided to begin the *Sheep Among Wolves* movement in Iran. In the days after Ayatollah Khamenei issued his fatwa against Christianity, the churches that appeared to be the strongest fell the fastest. The historic churches of Iran, with their illustrious history and their beautiful buildings, were easy targets for the government, which knew exactly where to find their leaders and how to shut down their services. Equally easy to extinguish were the Western-style churches, with their fancy websites and their boasting on social media. Most of these churches have never reopened their doors.

Meanwhile, in their weakness, the Iranian house churches were much more difficult to kill. The secret police had no idea where to find their leaders. If they raided a home where believers gathered, people simply started gathering elsewhere. The house churches looked very weak – with no website and no fixed assets – but this

---

1 This humbling process is not specific to the Seventy-Two. Jesus taught the same lesson earlier to the Twelve (Luke 9:3). This is a process through which each of us must pass in order to become fruitful in Jesus.

was why the secret police were left scratching their heads as to where they were and who were their leaders.

Furthermore, the weakness of the house-church leaders helped them to hide in plain sight. It was like the song in the Broadway musical *Les Misérables*: the government had no idea what our "little people" could do! One house-church leader had been a drug dealer and a computer hacker before he came to faith in Jesus. He showed the other leaders how to cover their trails by using fake IP addresses and burner phones, as well as how to slip away from police raids undetected. Another leader used to work for the morality police, patrolling the streets to reprimand any woman who wore lipstick and nail polish or who failed to wear the hijab properly. As a former insider, she knew how the secret police thought and was able to predict many of their moves.

Initially, the Iranian house churches remained hidden from Christians in the West. They were not on social media, so they went unnoticed. They were busy making disciples in their own country and responding to requests for them to coach underground church leaders in Afghanistan and in other neighboring nations. But then two important things happened. First, a team of American filmmakers asked if they could share the Iranian story with the world via a two-hour documentary entitled *Sheep Among Wolves: Part II*. Second, the COVID-19 pandemic shut down the churches of North America and Europe. Western Christians suddenly found themselves stuck at home.

During this global crisis, what the Iranians were learning about strength-through-weakness struck a chord with many people all around the world. The documentary notched up well over a million views during the pandemic. Church leaders in America and Europe began remarking that lockdown had shown them, too, that many of the people in their churches were converts rather than disciples. It was as if their people didn't know how to follow Jesus without being hand-held by their leaders. Like the Iranians, they noted that the strongest-looking churches were often hit the hardest.

Before COVID-19, *Sheep Among Wolves* was exclusively an Eastern movement, confined largely to the Islamic nations of the Middle East and Asia. Through the pandemic, it became a truly global movement. Many North American, European, African and South American believers began to forge connections with the Iranian believers, seeking to learn how to foster disciple-making movements of their own. If anybody had predicted, while the Iranian house churches were being ravaged by the secret police, that there would come a day when God would use them to train believers in the wealthy West, nobody would have believed it. But that's precisely what God has done. Through the pandemic, Jesus invited people all around the world to reflect on what his Forgotten Manifesto means for us today: "Do not take a purse or bag or sandals."

The COVID pandemic is now a thing of the past, but Western Christians are still left questioning whether the prevailing methods of church-planting are likely to succeed in re-evangelizing Europe and America. It requires such big budgets! First, you buy or rent a building. Then, you pay a pastor, even a whole staff team. Next, you develop infrastructures that look very similar to those of the churches that crumbled within the first few weeks of persecution in Iran. As a result, new churches can only be planted when sufficient money and manpower has been raised to support a complex program of ministries. All of this makes church-planting very slow. It is such a far cry from the willingness of Jesus to send his followers out in pairs with a promise that their weakness would become their superweapon.

God needed to strip Gideon down to size before he could use him. He stripped the Iranian leaders down to size too. So, how can you invite him to strip you down to size as well? The more you can ensure that all the glory will go to God for any breakthrough you encounter, the more you are likely to encounter breakthrough!

> **"The more you can ensure that all the glory will go to God for any breakthrough you encounter, the more you are likely to encounter breakthrough!"**

One of the tools we have discovered, for our teams both in the East and in the West, is to seek to serve God in places that are outside our comfort zone. Our natural tendency is to pursue *comfort*, *convenience* and *control*, so by deliberately ministering in places where we feel *uncomfortable*, *inconvenienced* and *out of control* we teach ourselves to rely much more on the Lord. For us, this has meant going to the red-light districts, to gambling dens and to gay bars – to the places where we are most likely to find "little people": the outcasts, the canceled, the rejected and the marginalized. It has meant going into mosques and temples and secular spaces to meet with militant Muslims and Hindus and atheists. It has led us to build friendships with disempowered ethnic groups and other sectors of society. One of the paradoxes of disciple-making movements is that the hardest places often yield the greatest results. Jesus loves to work through people who let him strip them down to size.

Another tool we have discovered is to take Jesus as literally as possible when he commands us, "Do not take a purse or bag or sandals." We seek to avoid setting up projects for people, because we inadvertently push away potential People of Peace whenever we cast ourselves in the role of helper. If we make people feel patronized (that we are better than they are) or infantilized (that they need our help because they cannot help themselves), they quickly respond by becoming passive. Going out into the harvest fields with nothing turns this on its head. When we approach potential People of Peace from a position of weakness, it is disarming and incredibly empowering.

**"When we approach potential People of
Peace from a position of weakness, it is
disarming and incredibly empowering."**

It was only because Jesus was thirsty that he was able to start up
a conversation with the Samaritan woman at the well. It was only
because he needed a fishing boat from which to preach that he was
able to invite Peter to take a first step toward partnering with him
in ministry. It was only because Jesus had nowhere to stay in Jericho
that he was able to invite himself to stay at the home of Zacchaeus.[2]
In the same way, we have discovered that stripping ourselves of our
own resources is one of the most effective ways of building bridges
with nonbelievers. It is the highly effective strategy of Jesus to help
us forge connections with People of Peace and to enlist them as
co-workers in the harvest fields.

Before you move on from this chapter, take a moment to reflect
on this:

- What is your current strategy for multiplying many more
  disciples across your nation?
- How well is that strategy working?
- If it isn't working, is that because you are too weak or because
  you feel too strong?

---

2   Luke 5:1–11, 19:1–10; John 4:7.

Iran: Meet some little leaders

People who meet the Iranian house-church leaders are often struck by how very ordinary they are. They discover the truth of 1 Corinthians 1, that God loves to do great things through "little people." We have therefore asked some of them to share their stories with you. We have changed their names to protect them from the secret police, and we have abridged their stories to make them a little easier for Christians in other nations to understand, but what you have here is a genuine cross-section of the early Iranian house-church leaders. These are the "little people" that God used to bring the revival to Iran in the years after Ayatollah Khamenei issued his fatwa.

Javed's story

I grew up on a farm in rural Iran. My father taught me how to take care of the land. He was a very wise man, and I still remember the most important thing he taught me: "God is the owner of the world and he is the one who blesses our land. Always turn to him, and to nothing else, for whatever you desire."

I was devastated when my father died. I had always looked up to him, and I wanted to be able to take care of our farm in a manner that would make him proud. However, a long drought made that impossible, and I was forced to sell the farm to become a taxi driver. I moved to a large city, far away from my family and friends, to make as much money as possible. I became so depressed. I woke up in tears almost every day, thinking about the wonderful life I used to enjoy in the countryside. I missed my father and his wisdom. I tried to numb the unbearable pain with alcohol and drugs. Quickly, my life began to unravel.

One night, I was alone in my bed, trying not to be completely overcome by my sadness. I stared at the ceiling, feeling lost and alone. Suddenly, in the quiet, I heard my father's voice: "Turn to God, and to nothing else, for whatever you desire." In that moment, I realized that I had been looking to other things. I fell to my knees and asked God to forgive me for turning to drugs and alcohol to find peace. I asked him, "Please change my life." It turned out that God was listening.

The very next day, I was sitting with a friend who was also a taxi driver. Two strangers came up to us and asked if they could join us. For some strange reason, I felt comfortable telling them my struggles and about how lost I was feeling. They both said that they had also reached a point in their lives where they felt the same way – but that God had changed everything for them. I knew right then and there that God was answering my prayer from the night before. I said to them, "God has sent the two of you to speak to me." They replied, "Yes, God told us to come and see you." The two men became my friends and helped me to read many stories from the Bible. With God's help, they enabled me to start living a new life, free from the drugs and alcohol. God began to heal me from the inside out, and soon I was no longer suffering from depression.

It is now my life's purpose to share these truths with others and to make the most of every opportunity I get to make disciples of the One True God. When I look back on my life, I praise God for how he prepared me to fulfill his purposes for my life. I no longer live on a farm, but God is definitely using me to plant seeds, just like my father. Only this time, it is to harvest a crop of believers from the seeds of salvation that I am sowing in their hearts.

Abdul's story

For much of my life I was motivated by fear. My parents and grandparents were extremely religious. They told me that I would never reach God unless I followed their Islamic rituals. Instead, I would be cursed and thrown into hell. For twenty-five years, I followed their religion to the letter. At times, I was genuinely hungry to reach the God they spoke about. At other times, I felt that their rituals were all meaningless and that I was merely following them out of fear. All the while, I was watching the turmoil and fighting that was going on in Iran in the name of their religion. I grew extremely disillusioned with Islam. I became confused and eventually slid into a state of depression.

That's when the True God came into my life. I befriended a man who seemed very different from anyone else I'd ever met. As we grew closer, he began to share some stories with me from the Bible. I learned about a God who deeply loves his children and who wants me to feel and share that love. This was nothing like the god of my parents and grandparents. This God was reachable. This God was available. This God loved me and wanted to have a genuine relationship with me. As I read more of the stories with my friend, it felt as though my mind and heart were brightened. I knew that I was finding the One True God.

Now I continue to seek God earnestly every day, but it is no longer an empty ritual. As I read the Bible, God deepens my understanding of who he is. I have found a new life of love, hope, honesty and joy. I am living in the loving embrace of my heavenly Father and I never want to leave.

I know that God has called me to share this embrace with others. I want everyone to know the loving and forgiving God who rescued me from a life of sin and who has given me a hope and a purpose for my future. I am now sharing with others the stories which my friend shared with me. God has turned my rituals into a relationship, and my fear into faith.

Nazanin's story

My mother suffered from mental illness and left home when I was very young. My brother physically abused me for many years, and I wasn't brave enough to fight back or to tell anyone. The only bright spot in my life was my father, whom I loved and who I knew loved me very much. His death was devastating, and I felt utterly abandoned and rejected.

In my hopelessness, I turned to a life of prostitution. When you have no sense of self-worth, it's not that hard to disregard your body and to use it to survive. I had lost any expectation of a future worth living for. I decided to set myself on fire so that my pain would finally disappear, but somebody called the firefighters. I felt such a failure. I couldn't even succeed in killing myself.

My body survived the fire but my soul was dead. I had no desire to live anymore, and I had nowhere to turn. Is this when we are most likely to hear God – when we have come to the end of ourselves and just want to give up and surrender? Well, that's how it was for me.

In my darkest hour, God sent two amazing women into my life. They wanted to know me and to help me. I found myself pouring out my heart to them, telling them everything that had happened to me and about my pain. They listened, they held my hand, and they told me there was another way to live. They told me about a man named Jesus and that he could replace my pain with peace. I had never heard anybody speak like this, with such love and hope. It felt almost as if this Jesus was the very person who was talking to me.

That night in my bedroom, I decided to talk to Jesus. As I stretched out my arms to him, I could feel the touch of someone reaching back, and I felt myself in the embrace of Jesus. The entire room was filled with his loving presence, and it was so powerful that I felt the desire to kneel down before him. With all the strength I could muster, I said, "Please don't leave me alone." In an instant, I knew for certain that he wouldn't, and that he would be with me forever.

From that point on, I couldn't learn quickly enough about God. Day and night I read stories about Jesus that my two new friends kept giving me. I discovered that he came to save me from sin and death. It was he who sent the firefighters to rescue me. I devoted myself to becoming a follower of Jesus. The women who came to talk to me were on a mission from God, and I know that I wouldn't still be here if they hadn't obeyed him. Now it is my turn to be like those women. I am on a mission for God, telling other women every day about the amazing love of Jesus Christ.

Leila's story

I have never had a very positive image of myself. I tried to find my self-worth in what other people thought of me. I married very young in the hope that I would find worth in my husband's eyes. Sadly, he had a terrible temper and would regularly beat me. When I finally decided to divorce him and go back to my family, my sense of self-worth plunged even lower. To my devoutly Muslim family, getting divorced was a taboo. My four brothers refused to let me leave the house. Becoming a prisoner in my own home made me feel like I could do nothing right and that I was unworthy of love from anyone, even from my family.

Eventually, I was able to persuade my brothers to let me get a job. This turned out to be the first step in an important journey. At my work, I met a kind lady. She was very warm and accepting and made me feel like I had something to offer the world. During our daily conversations, she started telling me stories about God. This was not the god I had heard about in my Muslim home, but the God of the Bible. I was very interested in what she had to tell me because she said that this God thought I was worthy of his love, so worthy that he had sent his Son, Jesus, to earth to die in my place so that I could have a relationship with him. Never before had I felt so loved and so accepted. All the shame I had been carrying from my failed marriage began to fall away and was replaced by the embrace of a forgiving God.

This message of forgiveness couldn't stop with me. I knew that I had to forgive my ex-husband and my family for the way they had treated me. Through forgiving them, I have experienced a freedom that can only come from God. I know that there are many other women out there who are struggling to find their worth in this life and who are turning to the wrong things, just as I was. Now I spend my time reaching out to them and trying to show them that they are worth more to the God who created them than they could ever imagine. I have been redeemed by the amazing God of the Bible and I will shout about his love to everyone forever.

These stories are brief, but the people are real. These are the "little people" God used to birth an exponential movement of disciple-makers in Iran. Hopefully two things will stand out to you.

First, that people are coming into a genuine relationship with the Lord Jesus. One of the great weaknesses of Islam is that it presents God as impersonal, distant and angry. There are ninety-nine names for Allah in the Qur'an, but none of them is "God is love." As a result of this, one of the common features of Iranian testimonies is that people marvel at the intimate friendship that they are able to experience with the Lord.

Second, that the Iranian disciples need this deep relationship with God because they know they would be nothing without Jesus. They accept that they are "little people" who have nothing in their hands except for the power of the gospel that is activated through their prayers.

They are like lambs among wolves. They are living proof that the Forgotten Manifesto of Jesus can prosper anywhere, at any time and with anyone.

5

Laser focus

Luke 10:4

"Do not greet anyone on the road." (Luke 10:4)

Jesus maintained a laser focus throughout his public ministry. On one occasion, after teaching and healing people late into the night at Peter's house, he got up early the next morning. His disciples woke up to find him gone. When they finally found him and informed him that crowds were gathering back at Peter's house, Jesus responded firmly: "Let us go somewhere else – to the nearby villages – so I can preach there also. That is why I have come" (Mark 1:3–8). Jesus never forgot the reason why the Father had sent him into the world. He never let the good things that he might have done distract him from completing the mission his Father had given him – modeling for his followers how to launch disciple-making movements all across the world. Jesus wouldn't even allow crowds of sick and hurting people to distract him from this laser focus for his public ministry.

Jesus is seeking to instill the same laser focus into the Seventy-Two when he commands them, "Do not greet anyone on the road." This is not an instruction for us to be rude to people, but for us to be laser-focused about our mission. We have learned the hard way that this is one of the most difficult battles for any would-be disciple-maker. When the devil sees that he can no longer stop us from obeying the Great Commission, he changes tactics. He switches to damage limitation instead. Having failed to prevent us from pursuing the Great Commission, he shifts his energy toward distracting us from pursuing it in a manner that will multiply disciples. Since the devil is laser-focused on distracting us from the Forgotten Manifesto of Jesus, we must be equally laser-focused on obeying it.

One of the reasons why it takes most people two to three years to see breakthrough in disciple-making movements is that they tend to get distracted by their old ways of doing things. The Iranian believers had seen thousands of conversions before the fatwa, so they kept on slipping back into their old methods of ministry. It took them five years to build momentum because their old habits died so hard. They kept on reverting to seeking to make converts through gospel presentations, instead of praying for God to reveal the People of Peace he was preparing in the harvest fields so that they could take them on a patient journey of discovery. The more fruitful we have been through our own methods of evangelism, the harder it seems to be for us to make the shift toward obeying the Forgotten Manifesto of Jesus. The devil loves to use our past to rob us of a better future. That's why God needs to do work *in* us before he can do his work *through* us.

Another reason why it takes most people two to three years to see breakthrough is that they get distracted into spending too much of their time mentoring existing Christians. We believe that we are part of the wider body of Christ and that we cannot say to any brother or sister, "I don't need you!" (1 Corinthians 12:21). However, one of the biggest paradoxes of disciple-making movements is that new believers tend to learn the principles of the Forgotten Manifesto of Jesus far faster than veteran Christians. We have found it far easier to train up a few hungry nonbelievers than to reinvigorate a larger group of half-hearted believers. We are committed to training up Christians who are hungry, but we cannot afford to waste our time with people who don't really want to change – not while there are so many genuine People of Peace waiting for us out in the harvest fields.

"We have found it far easier to train up a few hungry nonbelievers than to reinvigorate a larger group of half-hearted believers."

Jesus preached in the synagogues, but it's interesting that he made most of his disciples on the beaches and amid the crowds. The Apostle Paul announced his arrival in a new city by preaching at its Jewish synagogue, but it is obvious from his letters that the majority of his leaders were former pagans who had never darkened a synagogue door. While it might seem easier to gather nominal believers to attend a Bible study than it is to go out and find a group of nonbelievers, there are no shortcuts to disciple-making movements. Our goal is far bigger than launching Bible studies. It is helping nonbelievers to begin gathering together to read the Scriptures and to learn how to follow Jesus together. Backslidden Christians are easy to gather, but often for the wrong reasons. Some of them are flattered by the greater level of care and attention that they are offered by a house-church gathering. Others are attracted by the intellectual stimulation of deconstructing church with a group of like-minded friends. But unless they have a burning passion in their hearts to obey Jesus, and unless their hearts are breaking for the lost people around them, they will never become co-workers with us in the harvest fields. If you want to see a movement of disciple-makers reach your nation, then don't get distracted into gathering groups of existing Christians. Get out into the harvest fields. Stay laser-focused on obeying the command of Jesus in his Forgotten Manifesto: "Do not greet anyone on the road."

Some of the Christians we coach are happy to embrace the simple church structures of Luke 10 (meeting in houses) but not its missionary implications (looking for People of Peace who are ready to take their friends and family on a journey of discovery). Others are happy to look for People of Peace but seek to add them to their traditional church services. We have learned the hard way that those who seek to cherry-pick obedience to the Forgotten Manifesto are wasting our time and their own. Partial obedience to Jesus is disobedience in disguise. What would have happened to Peter if he had attempted to follow Jesus without leaving his old fishing nets behind? When people pursue a hybrid mixture of Luke 10 and traditional church methods, it doesn't work for them, and it becomes a distraction for us in our obedience to the Forgotten Manifesto.

> **"We have learned the hard way that those who seek to cherry-pick obedience to the Forgotten Manifesto are wasting our time and their own."**

In order to help ourselves to remain laser-focused, we have identified three key principles that we believe Jesus tells us need to underpin all of our groups and churches.

Everything needs to be **highly replicable**. To achieve this, we need to dial down our own gifting as leaders so that everything we do can easily be replicated by others. Disciple-making movements stall when gifted leaders subtly communicate that leadership requires an unusual amount of gifting. One of the great things about Discovery Groups is that they don't require facilitators who are gifted preachers or platform speakers. The bar for discipleship is set very high, but the bar for facilitating is set very low. We have found that releasing everyone to start and lead Discovery Groups is the best way of separating "talkers" from "walkers." Some of those who think they are gifted fail and flounder, while "little people" we might have overlooked become surprisingly fruitful.

Everything needs to be **highly autonomous**. It isn't just persecution that scatters those whose faith relies on centralized leadership structures. Even in peacetime, fast-growing centralized churches can be suffocated by problems of size. Jesus has commissioned us to make millions of disciples, and such growth is impossible through conventional command-and-control church leadership structures. We therefore aim for all our churches to be self-governing, self-correcting, self-funding and self-replicating. *Sheep Among Wolves* is not a denomination but a posture that binds together a group of like-minded friends. The only High Command we want our churches to have is the High Command of heaven.

Everything needs to be **highly obedient** to Jesus as Lord. Autonomy does not mean anarchy. It means helping people to hear the voice of Jesus and obey him. For this reason, we avoid becoming people's teachers. We facilitate discussions that train people to regard the Bible as the Word of God and the Spirit of God as their true teacher. Traditional approaches to disciple-making tend to focus on transferring large amounts of Christian knowledge, yet Jesus warns that his disciples are not marked by how much they know, but by how much they *obey*. God's "love language" toward us is mercy, and our "love language" toward God is trusting him enough to do whatever he says. Disciple-making isn't complicated. It means helping people to follow through on whatever insights God gives them into his will for their lives. One of our battle cries is "Death before disobedience!" Whenever we have failed to live up to this, we have become even more convinced that the true measure of a disciple of Jesus isn't how much we know, but how much we obey.

These three principles are helping us to remain laser-focused on following the Forgotten Manifesto of Jesus. If something is *highly replicable*, *highly autonomous* and *highly obedient* to Jesus, then it is healthy. If it isn't, then we know that we are doing something wrong.

Afghanistan: Khadija's story

The people at my church in my home country were surprised when I told them I had enrolled in a six-month training course with Youth With A Mission. They knew me as a shy girl who turned up faithfully but said very little. I wasn't exactly the kind of girl who was likely to go out and set the world on fire.

When I read in the newspaper that the Taliban were forbidding people from speaking about Jesus in Afghanistan, I knew very little about the country. I actually had to go and look on a map of the world to find out where it even was. But that same night I had a dream in which I saw God highlight Afghanistan on the map and tell me, "I want you to go there." I don't believe that the Lord spoke to me this dramatically because I'm special. I think that he just knew that, as a comfortable Westerner, I would never have gone to such a place unless he had made it really clear. Even after my dream, I tried to argue with God that I was the wrong person for him to send. I wasn't gifted at sharing the gospel in my own country, let alone in a strict Islamic nation.

My first few years in Afghanistan quickly confirmed this. Although I was able to show God's love to several Afghan women and to build strong friendships with them, whenever I tried to speak to them about Jesus those friendships ended abruptly. I began receiving death threats. A neighbor tried to poison me. On one occasion, somebody actually cut off and stole my hair! After six years of this, when the police detained me overnight in a prison cell, I finally had had enough. Several of my Christian friends had already been imprisoned or killed, and I feared that I was next. Coming to Afghanistan felt like a terrible mistake. I was on the brink of giving up and going home.

That's when I was introduced to the Iranian church leaders, who traveled into Afghanistan to train a group of us in what Jesus wants to teach us through Luke 10. I remember being struck by their commitment to prayer and fasting. They were obviously more interested in deepening our relationship with God than they were in promoting their own methodology. When they challenged us that we were chasing people away by speaking to them too quickly about Jesus, I was shocked but I was open to persuasion. They helped me to see that I was overloading people with too much of the gospel before they were ready to receive it. I recommitted my life to serving the Lord in Afghanistan, but this time with greater patience, prayer and fasting. I resolved to take people to the Scriptures and to trust the Holy Spirit to change their thinking over time, instead of expecting them to travel at my own speed.

I would love to tell you that everything changed overnight from that moment, but it took time. As I began to share stories from the Bible with Afghan women, I slowly started to see God touch their hearts in ways that I had never managed through my own powers of persuasion. Remember, I was the shy girl who was too scared to speak to people in my church back home! In time, I was able to lead some of the Afghan women to genuine saving faith in Jesus.

One example was a female security guard whose job was to search women for guns or explosives in the street near my home. "This feels like dangerous work," I sympathized with her. "Yes, but I don't have a choice. I need to work in order to help my family." When I asked her some questions, she opened up to me about her daughters. One of them was sick, so I used my Western contacts to buy her certain medicines which were in short supply. The other daughter seemed to be plagued by evil spirits, so I offered to pray for her. She was miraculously set free! Through this, I began to meet up regularly with the family to share stories from the Bible with them. As I took the security guard through the stories slowly, she confessed her sins and asked God to forgive her. She had found real peace with God and had begun sharing the Bible stories with her friends and family when she was killed by a bomb explosion. Her death was tragic, but I know she is with the Lord.

I have learned to be much more patient about how I share Jesus with people. If people are open to discussing stories from the Bible with me, then I begin with Creation and work very slowly toward Christ, trusting that the Lord will imprint enough truth on their hearts over several weeks for them to be saved. I was only three weeks into sharing the stories with one of my work colleagues when her brother was killed in an explosion. (Yes, there is sadly a lot of this kind of violence in Kabul.) We had only reached the story of the Fall in Genesis 3, but my work colleague had been going home and sharing each of the stories with her brother. The night before he was killed in the explosion, she shared the story of Adam and Eve with him. Before he went to bed, he prayed to God for forgiveness for his sins – not in the Islamic way of repeating Arabic phrases, but in a new and more personal way, confessing specific sins to the Lord. Before he left for work that fateful morning, he commented to his sister that he felt a supernatural peace when he prayed. When I think about what happened to him, I wonder what would have happened had I attempted to share more directly with my work colleague, as I used to when I first arrived in Afghanistan. I think she would have pushed me away. Even if she had listened, I doubt whether her brother would have been willing to listen to her stories second-hand. It was only because I was willing to be patient and to take her slowly from Creation to Christ that her brother was saved. Although the devil took him, he had become the Lord's.

In 2021, the Taliban came back into power in Afghanistan. I was in Iran at the time with some of the leaders there, so I could easily have used my Western passport to go back home. However, as I prayed, I felt the Lord recommission me to go back across the border. I explained to the Iranians that "Afghanistan is like a child inside of a burning building. God is calling me to be a mom who rushes in to save her child from the fire. Jesus did this for me, so how can I refuse to do it too?"

After I returned to Afghanistan, God used me to bring four people to faith in Jesus. We were able to form a little house church together in the capital city of the Taliban! These four new believers quickly began to reach out to others. Ten of their friends and family came to faith in Jesus too. They are now leading ten new house churches of their own. So, you see, the Lord has made me a spiritual great-grandmother! I came back into Afghanistan to be a mother to the nation, but now my spiritual children are having children and grandchildren of their own! It's hard to know how much is happening across Afghanistan right now, because we are meeting in secret, but it really seems to me that the Forgotten Manifesto of Jesus is working here. The beauty of a disciple-making movement is that it isn't about the strength of any human leader, but about the strength of the Lord. The Taliban are powerless to stop what God is doing through us.

I want to encourage you to believe that this is also true of your own country. The devil wants to tell you that "This won't work where you are," but that would be to think too little of our God. Whenever I travel back to the West, I find that there are People of Peace everywhere – the Christians around them are largely just not talking to them. I believe God has the same great plans for Western believers as he has for my friends and me in

Afghanistan. I believe he is calling them to stop staring at Netflix from the comfort of their couches and to open their eyes to the harvest fields around them.

God may not be calling you to move to Afghanistan, but he is calling you to be part of his disciple-making movement where you are. If he can do it through me, then he can do it through you!

6

People of Peace

Luke 10:5–6

"When you enter a house, first say, 'Peace to this house.' If someone who promotes peace is there, your peace will rest on them; if not, it will return to you." (Luke 10:5–6)

Jesus uses a phrase in Luke 10:6 that lies right at the heart of his Forgotten Manifesto. Jesus tells the Seventy-Two that God will answer their prayer for more co-workers by helping them to find many "People of Peace" within the harvest fields.

Some English Bibles find this phrase a little clunky, so they paraphrase it as "someone who promotes peace." This overlooks the fact that Jesus is using a Hebrew phrase from the Old Testament which denotes a "close friend" or a "key ally."[1] In the context of the Great Commission, it describes the new workers that God will motivate to join us in the harvest. How could the Twelve reach the whole of Galilee? How could the Seventy-Two reach the rest of Israel? How can we reach every nation of the world? Only by following the instructions of Jesus in his Forgotten Manifesto – by asking God to raise up many People of Peace within the harvest fields and to add them to our growing team of gospel workers.

Jesus commands the Seventy-Two to go into people's houses. They are not to hang out at the synagogues, hoping to enlist a group of believers. They are to hang out in the town square, making it

---

1 The Hebrew phrase "man of peace" is used in Psalm 41:9 and Jeremiah 20:10. The Greek phrase "son of peace" is used in Luke 10:6. We use the phrase "People of Peace" to reflect the fact that many of our best men of peace are women!

clear to everybody that they are visitors to town who can't afford to pay for a night at the inn. Self-sufficiency creates barriers between us and other people, but honest vulnerability draws the right people toward us. Lacking any purse or moneybag, it is easy for the Seventy-Two to flush out which of the townspeople are generous enough to welcome strangers into their home. Their weakness is their secret superweapon.[2]

> **"Self-sufficiency creates barriers between us and other people, but honest vulnerability draws the right people toward us."**

Jesus warns the Seventy-Two not to rush to share the gospel with those who welcome them into their homes. "Peace be to this house" was a very normal Jewish greeting – akin to the words *As-Salaam-Alaikum* across the Arab world today. The Seventy-Two should give a friendly greeting and allow their conversations over dinner to reveal whether or not their hosts are open to the message they have come to town to share.

This approach lies at the heart of disciple-making movements. We have learned to define a Person of Peace as *a nonbeliever who is willing to gather a group of nonbelievers to go on a journey of discovery with them*. To do this, they tend to be **open**, **hungry** and **quick to share**.

First, a Person of Peace is **open** with us about their struggles. They are welcoming toward us and honest with us about the challenges that they are facing in their lives.

Second, a Person of Peace is **hungry** for change. They don't accept that their struggles are here to stay. They are willing to do just about anything to see their life change.

---

2 For examples of this in action, see Genesis 19:1–3 and Judges 19:14–21. This is a far cry from the traditional missionary strategy of arriving in a new place with lots of money in order to start projects for the locals. It is also a far cry from organizing special services in sacred buildings and hoping nonbelievers will come along.

Third, a Person of Peace is **quick to share** what they learn with others. One of the earliest signs that God is raising them up to become our new co-worker is that they want their family and friends to join them in their journey to find out more about God. We want to help them to gather a Discovery Group, and this requires them to be quick to share.

Jesus modeled for us how to find People of Peace during his three years of public ministry. He arrived at the town of Sychar in Samaria without a bottle of water so that he could ask a woman to offer him a drink at the well. Although she was sinful, she was open with him about her struggles and expressed a hunger to see her life change. At the end of their conversation, she rushed off to share with her neighbors: "Could this be the Messiah?" Through that one conversation, the whole town of Sychar invited Jesus to stay with them for two more days. They told the woman: "We no longer believe just because of what you said; now we have heard for ourselves, and we know that this man really is the Savior of the world."

When Jesus moved on to the Decapolis region, on the far shore of Lake Galilee, he met a man tormented by a legion of demons. After driving out his demons, Jesus refused the man's request to join his traveling band of disciples. Instead, he commanded the man to "Go home to your own people and tell them how much the Lord has done for you." When Jesus returned to the Decapolis a few weeks later, crowds of locals flocked to see him. Jesus shows us how one Person of Peace is able to open up a whole community to the gospel.[3]

"Jesus shows us how one Person of Peace is able to open up a whole community to the gospel."

---

3   John 4:1–42; Mark 5:1–20, 7:31 – 8:1.

Jesus only had 120 loyal followers by the time he ascended back to heaven, yet he was able to report back to his Father that "I have brought you glory on earth by finishing the work you gave me to do" (John 17:4). That's a remarkable conclusion! After three years of recruiting 120 People of Peace, Jesus considered his own work to be finished. His team of willing workers would now take things on from here.

In the book of Acts, those willing workers follow the Forgotten Manifesto. Peter prays and watches as God forges a miraculous connection between him and a Roman centurion named Cornelius. When Peter enters the man's home, he finds it crammed full of nonbelievers who want to go on a journey of discovery with Cornelius. The man is *open* and *hungry* and *quick to share*. Peter was the first to preach the gospel to a large group of Romans, but it was Cornelius who gathered them and then went on to disciple them.

Paul followed the same strategy to reach the Greek city of Philippi. He prayed and then watched as God helped him to forge miraculous connections with three people from very different sectors of the city. The businesswoman Lydia quickly gathered a group of well-to-do citizens in her home. The slave-girl whom Paul delivered from a demon was able to share her story with the poor and downtrodden. The jailer whose life Paul saved was quick to share with his family, and they were all baptized together. Since he was neither rich nor poor, the jailer could reach the everyday people of Philippi. By finding these three People of Peace, Paul was able to reach every sector within the city of Philippi.[4]

This is how Paul was able to conclude in Romans 15:23 that "there is no more place for me to work in these regions." He had only planted a few small churches in a handful of key cities in the Eastern Mediterranean, yet since his task was to find People of

---

4   Acts 10:9–48, 16:13–34, 16:40.

Peace, his work was done. A few years later, he was able to write to many believers in the region "who have not met me personally" (Colossians 2:1). Paul followed the Forgotten Manifesto of Jesus, seeking out People of Peace in every place to become his co-workers in the harvest fields.

When the Iranians grasped this principle by studying Luke 10, it felt as though a massive weight fell off their shoulders. For the first time, the Great Commission felt achievable. If the Lord promises to empower us to find thousands of People of Peace, then reaching millions of nonbelievers is not beyond us. There is no limit to how many people we can reach with the good news. All we need to do is to engage with as many groups of lost people as possible, praying that the Lord will forge miraculous connections between us and the People of Peace he is raising up to join us in the harvest fields. We are then to help them to begin Discovery Groups, which will become Multiplying House Churches. At the heart of all of this lies the principle of **insider ministry**.

Insiders spread the gospel much more rapidly. One of the reasons why we struggle to reach nonbelievers is that we don't belong to their tribe. They do not accept us, because they don't know us and because we don't speak their language or understand their culture. This is as true of social groups as it is of ethnic groups. Societies consist of "affinity groups," small silos of people, each of which needs to be reached with the gospel. When adults seek to reach teenagers or when rich people seek to reach the poor, they find it hard to gain traction, but a Person of Peace already belongs to the unreached affinity group. They do not need to spend years learning the language or studying the culture or building strong relationships. They possess all of those advantages already. That's why the gospel always spreads more quickly through less gifted insiders than it can through a gifted outsider.

"The gospel always spreads more quickly through less gifted insiders than it can through a gifted outsider."

Traditional evangelistic methods seek to draw new converts out of their communities and into a church family. The devil loves this. He has worked hard in the Middle East to persuade people that "Christian" equals "foreign." When we encourage new believers to leave behind their Muslim families and friends, it alienates instead of winning their community. It is a case of *one won for Jesus and nine safeguarded for Satan*, and those are odds that the devil is happy to play all day! The Forgotten Manifesto of Jesus teaches us to help new believers to remain within their social networks, instead of leaving them. It makes it possible for it to be a case of *ten won for Jesus and none left for Satan*.[5]

Insiders commend the gospel much more clearly. When we help People of Peace to remain within their affinity groups, then their family and friends witness the changes that the Holy Spirit is working in their lives. An example of this in the Middle East is the way that male believers start to treat the women in their lives. In Iran, the legal age at which a girl can marry is thirteen. Women are required by law to hide their hair in public, and many of them feel they are regarded as second-rate to men. When men discover through our Bible stories that God created men and women to be equal, as his image bearers, and that Jesus honored women, it changes how they live at home. We don't want to hide people's light under a bushel by taking them out of their families and their affinity groups. It is irresistibly attractive to those around them, so we want their light to shine! The result is what Jesus led us to expect when he promised his followers that their new disciples would

---

5 Paul insists in 1 Corinthians 7:20 that "Each person should remain in the situation they were in when God called them." In the book of Acts, God invariably saves families and friendship groups, not isolated individuals.

"produce a crop – some thirty, some sixty, some a hundred times what was sown" (Mark 4:20).

When the Iranian believers began working across the border in Iraq, they didn't fully grasp this principle. They led a beautiful couple to faith in Jesus and connected them with a Western-style church so that they could be discipled. Within months, the couple's families were very hostile toward them. Their village leaders told them that they were no longer welcome to come home. We weep when we imagine what God might have done throughout that whole community had we not extracted these People of Peace upon conversion, but instead had done what Jesus tells us in his Forgotten Manifesto.

Insiders distribute the workload much more evenly. Missionaries talk about the "choke effect" of gospel breakthrough. It takes them so long to disciple their first batch of converts that further outreach has to take a backseat for a while. By promising the Seventy-Two that he will turn their converts into co-workers, Jesus eliminates this "choke effect." Instead, he pledges to redeem the existing leadership structures within affinity groups and to set them to work on behalf of the gospel. Husbands and wives will lead their families to faith in Jesus.[6] Those families will then reach out to their friends. A Person of Peace is our gateway into an affinity group, which becomes our gateway into the wider community.

It helps if a Person of Peace comes to faith in Jesus quickly, but even if they don't, we find that they are able to take their friends and family on a journey of discovery with them. The Bible teaches us that the gospel is powerful, not because of any human teacher, but because of the Lord. The Spirit of God longs to speak to people through the Word of God (John 14:26; 1 Timothy 3:14–17). It

---

6 It isn't just husbands who lead their wives to the Lord. We encourage Women of Peace to ask their husbands to explain the meaning of the Bible stories that we share with them. As they ask their husbands the same seven simple questions that we ask them, they prove the truth of 1 Peter 3:1–6. There is no greater advert for the gospel than a husband witnessing God's Spirit transforming his wife through God's Word.

therefore doesn't matter who places the seed of the gospel in people's hearts. Believer or nonbeliever, it is God who makes the seed grow.

Therefore, when we look for People of Peace and foster insider ministry, the Great Commission becomes achievable. We find that we are able to make disciples of all nations.

"When we look for People of Peace and foster insider ministry, the Great Commission becomes achievable."

Iran: Meet some People of Peace

The command of Jesus to look for People of Peace lies right at the heart of his Forgotten Manifesto. You need to grasp this clearly if you want to see a rapid advance of the gospel across your nation. The idea that nonbelievers can help us to lead other nonbelievers to faith in Jesus represents such a radical change of thinking that it takes most people a while to get their heads around it. To help you, I want to introduce you to some of the beautiful People of Peace the Lord added to his team of harvesters in order to spread the gospel across Iran. My prayer is that, as you read these stories, God will help you to believe in his promise to give you many such People of Peace where you are.

Mahmud's story

I am a jeweler and a watchmaker. I am good at my job, but sadly I was not as good at being a husband. My wife loved me deeply but I didn't love her. I turned to drugs and alcohol to satisfy me, but instead of helping me, they drained my money and almost made me lose my store. I hit rock-bottom when I discovered that my son had followed my example by becoming an addict too. I didn't know where to turn.

That's when I met two strangers who began to tell me stories about God. I was eager to listen, because I had always been curious about God but had never really known where to go to find out more about him. The more the two men told me, the more I wanted to know. I began to read their stories over and over, and eventually learned that they were stories from the Bible.

It is hard to describe what happened during this time. As I read and reread their stories, it seemed that God seized my heart, and I began to desire to be obedient to him. When we finally reached the stories about Jesus, I felt like a veil had been lifted from over my eyes. I began to believe what I was discovering – that God loves me and that he has a specific plan in mind for my life. The first part of this plan was for me to have a loving marriage. God literally changed my heart and I began to fall in love with my wife. After forty years of marriage, I told her that I loved her – for the first time ever! Then God moved my wife's heart, and she came to know Jesus as her Lord and Savior too. In his great mercy, God also freed our son from his drug addiction.

Looking back, it is clear to me now that God was always pursuing me – I just was unaware of it until I met my two new friends. God has always been with me, through the good times and the bad. Now that he has finally captured my heart, I only want to live for him and his plan for my life. My wife and I are sharing the Bible stories we have learned with everyone we know because we want them to discover the same truth as us – that God loves them and has a purpose for their lives. Many of the people we have shared with have now come to faith in Jesus too.

Sahar's story

As one of eight children, my parents expected me to work from a young age to help them put food on the table for my brothers and sisters. Sadly, they made some very bad choices. My father's drug addiction and poor investments took our family into debt we could not repay. I began to work a second job, but even that was not enough. People do things in desperate situations, and my parents forced me to begin a sexual relationship with my boss in return for money. It's hard to describe what happens inside your mind when you do such things. At first, I was upset and angry. I told myself this would only be for a short time until we were out of debt. But steadily, I stopped caring. I felt so ashamed of who I had become.

I took the bus home from work every day. One evening, I heard two women in the seats next to me talking about a gathering that they were going to in someone's home. One of them caught my attention when she remarked to her friend that "The women at these gatherings are really loved by God." When I heard this, I could feel my heart begin to pound in my chest. I wanted to know this kind of love. I wanted to feel God hug me and tell me everything was going to be OK. I summoned the courage to ask the women if I could join them and they happily said, "Yes." I met many women that night, but two in particular spent time talking with me and asked if I would give them my phone number. The next day, they called me and asked if they could come and see me. I was thrilled. They spent time teaching me about God through stories in the Bible. I listened to them intently, and I heard so much more than their voices. I heard a voice that I knew was God. He said, "You wanted to be hugged by me. I sent these two women to you so that you could feel my love. I am reaching out through them to hug you."

As I continued to study stories from the Bible with my new friends, my understanding of God deepened. He gave me the strength to make some very difficult decisions. As an act of obedience, I quit my prostitution and began to trust in God to be the true Provider for my family. I am so grateful that God used a bus ride to change my life. I now feel God's hug every day, and I am working hard to share that same hug of God with as many other people as I can.

Parvez's story

There are things that get passed down from our parents – both good and bad. I came from a good family and I loved my parents very much. Like many children, I wanted to please them and to make them proud, so I did my best to follow their beliefs and practices. However, when I tried to say their Islamic prayers, it didn't seem to work for me. I felt dissatisfied and disappointed, which ultimately led to feelings of guilt. I carried on feeling like this well into my adult life.

I owned a store in the city where I lived. One evening a customer came in and, as I was helping him, we struck up a conversation. We seemed to have many things in common, and soon the conversation turned to religion. I learned that he had experienced some of the same struggles that I had, yet he shared with me that he had been able to find peace with God. As he shared his journey with me, I was astonished by what I heard. The man evidently had a personal relationship with God, something I had given up thinking was even possible.

When I asked the customer to explain further, he told me that he had learned to know God by reading some sacred stories. I asked him if he would share these stories with me. As I read the stories with him, I began to understand that they were a revelation of the One True God. I had been seeking after a false god named Allah, but the God of the Bible was real. He wanted to have a relationship with me, and I was eager to respond. So eager, in fact, that I shared these stories with my wife, my sister and my three best friends. How could I keep such amazing news to myself?

As I asked God to speak to me through the Bible stories, it soon brought something else: conviction. One of the stories that I read spoke about the importance of forgiveness. This struck me deeply, and I knew that I was being prompted by the Holy Spirit to deal with the unforgiveness I felt in my heart toward my grandfather. He had caused many problems for our family over the years and, even though he had already died, I knew that

I needed to forgive him for all of the harm he had caused us. I didn't want to do it, but I knew that it was something God was telling me to do. I put aside my pride, went to my grandfather's tomb and, through God's grace, I was able to forgive him. All the pain and hate I felt toward him left my heart that day.

Now that I have experienced the beauty of a personal relationship with God, my only regret is that I didn't find him sooner. I don't want a single person on this planet to feel the way I did before I knew God, so I will share the good news about Jesus with everybody all the days of my life.

Alperen's story

I was always brought up to work hard. My oldest memories, even as a child, are of me working. My parents were older than my friends' parents, so from a young age I became responsible for supporting my family financially. I usually held several jobs at once, but as my income grew so did my problems. In a small village like mine, there weren't a lot of options for me to spend my extra cash. This is where my drug addiction was born. My mother's cure for this was to find me a husband, but after that my drug abuse got even worse. In less than two years, I found myself divorced, embarrassed, ashamed and alone.

Once again, my mother decided that marriage was the answer to my problems. I married for a second time, left my small village behind and moved to the capital, Tehran. Once again, my mom was wrong. I fought constantly with my new husband. I had distanced myself from everyone and I felt so alone. I realized that I had pushed away everyone who had ever tried to get close to me – even God. In a moment of desperation, I cried out to him: "God, please save me from this life because I feel like I am losing everything all over again."

Soon after this, one of my friends with whom I used to do drugs came to speak to me about God. My friend's life had been changed, and he shared with me that mine could be changed too. I prayed to God, "If this is true, take away my addiction to these pills." As my desire to know more about God grew and grew, my friend was there to show me stories in the Bible about who God is and about what he can do. The more stories he told me, the clearer my picture of God became. Knowing about God is one thing, but actually *knowing* God is what transforms us. God took away my desire for drugs. God healed my marriage. God revealed to me that he sent Jesus to be my Lord and Savior. God also gave me a passion to share these same stories with others. When you experience the redeeming power of Jesus, it is impossible not to share.

Recently, I sensed God calling me to leave Tehran and go back to my village to share these truths with all the people I grew up with. I want them to know the healing power of Jesus and the forgiveness he offers to all people. It isn't proving easy, but as I told you, I was always brought up to work hard. My ability to work hard has never been as important as it is right now.

Parbeen's story

I was pretty well versed in religion. I visited many of the sacred sites of Iran and performed all of the Islamic ceremonies that I was told would bring me close to God – but it was useless. My life felt empty and meaningless and, when your life is empty, you try to fill it up with something. I turned to alcohol and promiscuous relationships, but it didn't satisfy my longings.

It was during an ordinary visit to the beauty salon that something extraordinary happened. There was a woman there who was quite a bit older than me. She was sitting quietly, reading a book, and something made me feel drawn to her. I couldn't put my finger on it but nor could I shake off the feeling that I should talk to her – so I did. I found myself telling her all my secrets. Looking back, I can see how important the timing of this conversation turned out to be, because I was about to lose everything when my house caught fire and burned down to the ground. I was devastated and had no idea how to start rebuilding my life again. This is how I know that God was watching over me. He had already sent somebody to help me through that traumatic time.

The lady at the salon helped me by sharing stories with me about God. They weren't like any stories I had heard before at the Islamic shrines. These were about a loving God who knew me and loved me and had a plan and purpose for my life. I discovered that these were stories from the Bible and that God has a Son named Jesus Christ. As I reread the stories on my own, I began to see Jesus all around me, working in my life, and I asked him to become my Lord and Savior. I gave up my drinking and my promiscuity and, as I obeyed God, I saw him bless me over and over again.

My friend was a disciple-maker, and now I have become a disciple-maker too. I host Bible discussions in my home, where I have already seen one of my good friends place her own faith in Jesus. I share the same Bible stories with the people I meet throughout the day, and now I have seen six of them come to know the Lord Jesus through our conversations. I am so grateful that God has given me an eternal meaning to my life: that of bringing more people to know him. I know that this is just the beginning, and I am ready, always and forever, to be on a mission to change the world for him.

Meet some People of Peace

These are some of the amazing people God has used to spread the gospel across Iran. They are living proof of what Jesus promises he will do for us if we follow his Forgotten Manifesto. If we pray for more workers and if we go out in faith for God to answer our prayers by leading us to People of Peace, then we will find that he enables us to reach the lost millions in our nations.

7

Go slow to go fast

Luke 10:5–6

"When you enter a house, first say, 'Peace to this house.' If someone who promotes peace is there, your peace will rest on them; if not, it will return to you." (Luke 10:5–6)

You don't have to be a relationships expert to know that it causes problems when we come on too strong with people. If you spend a first date talking about how many children you want and which color you have chosen for your bridesmaids' dresses, then you probably won't get a second date on which to apologize. The Forgotten Manifesto of Jesus warns us that, when it comes to finding People of Peace, it can be the same. Jesus teaches us not to come on too strong too early. He warns us that we need to learn to go slow to go fast.

Jesus models this for us in the gospels. Note how guarded he was with people in the towns and villages he visited. When they asked, "If you are the Messiah, tell us," he did not respond, "You bet I am." Instead, he shot back: "If I tell you, you will not believe me."

When they urged him to clarify, "Who is this 'Son of Man'?" he did not say, "Isn't it obvious? It's me!" Instead, he warned them, "You are going to have the light just a little while longer. Walk while you have the light, before darkness overtakes you."

When they asked him, "Where is your Father?", he did not say, "He is in heaven." He replied: "You do not know me or my Father." When they became impatient – "How long will you keep us in suspense? If you are the Messiah, tell us plainly" – he refused to be hurried. "I did tell you, but you do not believe. The works I do in my Father's name testify about me."[1]

Jesus taught his followers to be equally careful not to blurt out his identity to people. We are frequently told that "He ordered his disciples not to tell anyone that he was the Messiah," and told the demons to be silent "because they knew who he was."[2] Jesus models for his disciples how to find People of Peace by sharing the good news at an appropriate speed. When he commissions the Twelve, he doesn't tell them to proclaim his divinity or his plan to die on a cross for the sins of the world. He commands them to pique people's curiosity by giving them a mysterious promise that "The kingdom of heaven has come near" (Matthew 10:7).[3] When Jesus commissions the Seventy-Two, he teaches them to do the same. "When you enter a house, first say, 'Peace to this house.'" Since this was the normal Jewish greeting – *Shalom!* – Jesus is warning them not to blurt out too much truth to people too early. They must lead them on a journey of discovery, which means learning to go slow to go fast.

The wisdom of this is obvious in Iran and Afghanistan. Talking to people about Jesus too early can get a Christian killed. Taking people on a journey of discovery gives them time to sniff out members of the secret police and to gauge how open people are to the gospel before they share too much of it with them. But we have learned the wisdom of this command in Western nations too. While we may not be arrested for proclaiming the gospel in America or Europe, using trigger words such as "church" or "Christianity" or "Jesus" too early in a conversation tends to provoke nonbelievers to pull away from us. They may be polite

---

1   Luke 22:67; John 8:19, 10:24–25, 12:34–35.

2   Matthew 16:20, 17:9; Mark 1:24–25, 1:34, 3:11–12, 8:30, 9:9; Luke 9:21.

3   Jewish people knew about the kingdom of God from their Old Testament Scriptures, but very few of them could say what it signified. We are to tap into similar spiritual mysteries within our own culture.

enough to carry on the conversation, but there is a look in their eyes which betrays that they have jumped to all sorts of conclusions about us. They are no longer open to receiving the good news that we long to communicate to them.[4]

Jesus does not tell us to go slow to go fast in order to keep us safe. He says it to help us be successful in our mission. Jesus explains his motivation in John 6:44, when he tells us that "No one can come to me unless the Father who sent me draws them." People need time to process the different elements of the gospel, so if we push them to accept too much truth in a single conversation, we may find ourselves running ahead of what God is doing in their hearts. By teaching them too much too early, we get in the way of the Holy Spirit becoming their true teacher. Consider how Jesus imparts faith to his disciples in Matthew 16:13–20.

Jesus is two years into his three years of public ministry. It has taken him this long to sense that his disciples are ready for the Holy Spirit to reveal his true identity to them. "Who do people say the Son of Man is?" he asks initially, knowing that a question about what other people think can feel less threatening than a direct question about ourselves. Jesus follows this up with a second, more penetrating question: "What about you? Who do you say I am?" Peter replies, "You are the Messiah, the Son of the living God." Jesus tells him: "Blessed are you, Simon son of Jonah, *for this was not revealed to you by flesh and blood*, but by my Father in heaven [my italics]."

Jesus is flesh and blood, so he is stating here that Peter's understanding of the gospel has not come from his own skill as a disciple-maker. He didn't reveal this truth to Peter, because he didn't want to convert people through the strength of his own flesh and blood. Instead, he made space for his Father to reveal truth to people through his Holy Spirit. How much more, then, must we? When we cast ourselves in the role of teacher, we get in the way of the Holy

---

4 Matthew 7:6 is as much a warning from Jesus to Christians in the West as it is to Christians in the East.

Spirit teaching people. It is desperately self-defeating. What's more, we prevent what we are doing from being replicable. Since our aim is to convince People of Peace that they can lead their friends to faith in Jesus just as readily as we can, we need to ensure that everything we do appears simple enough for everybody else to imitate.

> **"Jesus made space for his Father to reveal truth to people through his Holy Spirit. How much more, then, must we?"**

We cannot overemphasize the importance of going slow to go fast. It isn't just a tactic to protect believers in countries where sharing the gospel openly is likely to get them killed. It is also how Jesus teaches his followers to reach people in free countries, since coming on too strong with people robs them of their willingness to listen. We have distilled down what Jesus teaches us here into the "7 Ss" of how to share the gospel effectively with people (see Figure 7.1).

We start **simple**, by speaking whatever the equivalent of "Peace to this house" is to each person in their culture. With men, the simplest conversation starter seems to be asking them a question about sport or news or politics. With women, it is normally more effective to compliment an item of jewelry or clothing and to ask where they bought it. Let's not be insincere about this. We really do want to become their new best friends! Since we never know which of the people around us are People of Peace, let's be the friendliest people in our neighborhoods, engaging with as many different people as possible. Our aim is not to notch up a certain number of gospel conversations, but to find out who is warm and welcoming toward us. We do this by loving and listening to people.

Next, we seek to transition the conversation onto things more **serious**. We look for ways to ask deeper questions about the person's work or life or family. With some people this happens straightaway. With others it may take several interactions, which is why we

SIMPLE

⋁

SERIOUS

⋁

SPIRITUAL

⋁

STRUGGLE

⋁

SIFT

⋁

STORIES

⋁

SUPERNATURAL ENCOUNTER

Figure 7.1 The "7 Ss" – seven stages in a go-slow-to-go-fast gospel conversation

need to frequent the same stores and coffee shops to build deeper relationships with people over time. We get to know their names and we take a lead in being vulnerable with them. When we share with them openly about the struggles in our own lives, we may find that they open up to us too. Proverbs 20:5 likens this type of conversation to lowering a bucket down into a well in order to draw out the deep waters of people's hearts.

From there, we try to turn the conversation toward things

spiritual. We don't do this by whipping out a pen and paper and drawing a gospel diagram. We simply ask questions about what makes them tick at their deepest level. What do they think life is all about? Where do they tend to go with their struggles? Do they ever pray? How did they develop their faith or their lack of faith? In all of this, we avoid religious jargon and trigger words. We show our love to people by speaking their language and by listening to what they say.

> ## "We show our love to people by speaking their language and by listening to what they say."

Through these simple-serious-spiritual conversations, we invite people to share with us whatever **struggle** they are currently facing[5] (see Figure 7.2). One person's struggle is *emotional*. They open up to us about their anger or loneliness or anxiety or grief or shame. Another person's struggle is *relational*. They confide in us that they are experiencing rejection or abuse or bullying. Another person's struggle is *mental*: an addiction, or a battle with depression or suicidal thoughts. The next person's struggle is *physical*: a disability or sickness, or challenges of debt or unemployment. Another person's struggle is *spiritual*: a sense of emptiness or fear, or trouble they suspect may be caused by evil spirits. Everybody's struggle is different. What we are seeking at this stage is simply for the person to be open with us about their problems. This may be a sign that we are talking with a Person of Peace, whose heart the Lord has already prepared for us.

To find out for sure, we ask more questions that **sift** things further. A Person of Peace is someone who is *open* about their struggles, *hungry* for things to change, and *quick to share* whatever they learn with others. We therefore help our new friend to articulate their struggle in their own words, being as specific as possible. We have

---

5   This is what Jesus is seeking to do in the gospels when he asks potential People of Peace, "What do you want?" (Luke 18:41; John 1:38). He is effectively asking them, "What is going on in your life and how can I help?"

Emotional	Relational	Mental
Anger	Conflict	Addiction
Anxiety	Betrayal	Depression
Shame / Guilt	Rejection	Hopelessness
Sadness	Abuse	Suicidal thoughts
Divorcing parents	Marriage issues	Disappointment
Bereavement	Longing for love	Self-loathing

Physical	Spiritual
Overeating	Emptiness
Smoking	Lack of purpose
Health issues	Dissatisfaction
Disability	Fear
Lack of job or career	Tormented thoughts
Poverty	Encountering demons
Homelessness	Trapped by the occult
Debt	Worried about eternity
Trapped in the country	Longing to know God

Figure 7.2 **Common struggles**

learned not to counsel them or offer to pray for them at this stage in the process, since we want to offer them more than momentary relief. We express our love for them by turning their struggle into a springboard by which they can dive into a journey of discovery. We ask them, "How much do you want to overcome this struggle?" If their answer is noncommittal, we move on, since God has not yet done a deep enough work in their hearts for us to be able to help them. If their answer reveals real desperation, then we get excited, since that may indicate that the Lord has led us to a Person of Peace, a new co-worker in the harvest fields.

Now and only now do we offer to share some of our life-changing **stories** with them. We encourage our new friend that "There is a discovery process that has changed our lives and that is changing people's lives all around the world. Could we share it with you?" Even at this stage, we may not reveal that the stories come from the Bible. We continue to go slow to go fast.

Our goal in all of this is to bring people to a place where God can begin speaking to them by his Spirit through his Word. We are convinced that it is by reading or listening to Bible stories that people have a **supernatural encounter** with God. We make disciples by connecting people with God's Spirit through God's Word, so we have learned not to scare off people prematurely from setting out on a journey of discovery with us.

Take a moment to reflect on how these "7 Ss" are different from your own current way of sharing the gospel with people. Are you succeeding in leading nonbelievers to saving faith in Jesus? If you are not, could it be that you are scaring them away? If you are succeeding, what happens to people after they pray the sinner's prayer with you? Do they go the distance and become disciples who multiply more disciples? Or do they fall away?

These are some of the questions Jesus addresses through his Forgotten Manifesto. He warns us not to come on too strong with people. We need to learn to go slow to go fast.

America: Robert's story

I have been involved in the Church for many years, first as a youth pastor, then as lead pastor, planting or helping to plant several churches. I love the Church, but I've always sensed we were made for more. Most of our energy was spent on preaching sermons, having a "killer band," being out in the community doing "random acts of kindness" that demonstrated God's love to people, and giving them a church card inviting them to one of our services.

The Lord used the COVID-19 lockdown to make me take a long hard look at what we were doing. Despite our efforts, it didn't seem to cross the minds of those we helped that they should ever actually take us up on our invitation. I came to see that this was because the way we were trying to reach them wasn't vulnerable. It was transactional. We gave them help and in return they took our church cards. They regarded our projects as a church marketing campaign.

I spent a lot of the pandemic praying, asking the Lord to show me how he wanted us to reach people with the gospel. It couldn't be what we were doing, because Jesus told parables about the kingdom of God being like a fast-growing seed, or like yeast quickly working its way through a large batch of dough. That wasn't our experience at all, so I cried out for the Lord to show me a better way.

By God's grace, during lockdown I managed to connect with the *Sheep Among Wolves* believers online. I had watched the documentary on YouTube, so I knew about the revival in Iran. What I didn't realize at the time was that the gospel movement in Iran had started spreading to many other nations of the world. One of the Iranian leaders took the time to coach me patiently as I studied Matthew 10 and Luke 10, seeking to rediscover the Forgotten Manifesto of Jesus. At the end of several weeks and months, the lights came on. I saw why so much of what we tried before wasn't working. I felt God say to me, "I no longer want you to invite people to the building. I want you to invite them into a relationship with me and you!" By the time the pandemic ended, I felt ready to go out and give the "7 Ss" approach a try.

At first, I didn't find it easy. I had spent so many years blurting out the gospel too early to people that I found myself doing it again and again. I would say the word "church" or "Christianity" or "Jesus" too early and watch as people instinctively put their barriers up against me. I refer to this traditional evangelism approach as "one-and-done." You try to cram everything you have to say to a person about God into one single conversation, and by the time you have finished they are done talking to you forever! It is very different from the disciple-making approach that Jesus teaches us in Luke 10, which is all about building relationships with people.

God was giving me a paradigm shift in how he wanted me to interact with people. Through prayer and practice, it has become like second nature for me to do things the way that Jesus did. Something clicked, and it was as if I had discovered what I was always made for. I have never felt more alive! Now I start up simple conversations in a friendly and authentic way with people. I say, "Hey, man, how's your day going?" and then I listen. Instead of focusing on what I want to say to people, I try to focus on showing them that I care.

As we begin to get to know each other better, I try to shift the conversation onto something a little bit more serious. My aim is for them to open up to me about their struggles, so my motto is: "I go first at being vulnerable." I might share how, several years ago, I went through a process of recovery to deal with an addiction. It was the hardest and most difficult time in my life, but now I rarely think about it. It's almost as if it was another life. Or I might say: "I know what it's like to have all this pressure to live up to other people's expectations." This enables me to go on to say: "Do you mind me asking: Is there anything you're struggling with or any challenges you're facing right now?" Not one of the hundred-plus people I have asked that question to over the past few months has come up with a blank. Everybody has something. People are starving for a safe place to be real. We just have to learn to ask them the right questions in the right way. Our old "one-and-done" approaches rarely do this. We need to aim instead at building a relationship with the person that will continue. I'm amazed at how people are willing to be real with me about their struggles.

I have had to train myself not to respond to people's troubles with helpful advice. I don't want to give them comfort for a brief moment. I want to harness the momentum that their struggle is creating in their life to catapult them toward a relationship with God. For the same reason, I don't tend to pray with people about their struggles – at least not at first. I want to help them find a long-term solution to their struggles through faith in God, and faith in God comes by reading his Word, so instead I ask people, "On a scale of 1 to 10, if you could be free from that struggle, how badly would you want that?" Most people answer with a 10. A few even give me a 15 or a 20!

Since they seem open, I try to transition them into reading some stories from the Bible with me by saying to them, "I would love to share a process with you that has changed my life and is changing people's lives all over the world. Would it be OK if I shared that process with you?" Most people give me permission to go further, so I tell them: "It starts with asking: What are we thankful for?" I always go first, to give them time to think and to show them what I mean by the question. Then I say, "It continues by asking: What are we struggling with?" I go first again, then I give them time to restate their struggle to me in their own words, being as specific as they can.

If things are going well, I share a sample story with them. I tend to use Psalm 23 because its first line is "God is my shepherd. He makes sure that I lack nothing." This gives me a chance to introduce the idea that God is the one who is able to resolve their struggle, while demonstrating what a Discovery Bible Study looks like. I have the psalm on my phone so I tend to read a line or two of it at a time, asking them each time: "What does this tell you about God? What does it tell you about yourself?" Then I close by asking the person, "Reading this together, what jumps out to you as something that you want to focus on changing this week?"

The whole process has taken us less than twenty minutes and it has felt natural. I haven't asked them to listen to a long gospel presentation. I have taken them to the Scriptures and I have asked them a few questions. I have spoken way less than they have, trusting in the Holy Spirit to use the Word of God to teach them. As a result, when I ask them, "How did you like that? Would you like to do it again?", they usually say how much they loved it. They find it so open and so easy to engage with.

In the past month, I have begun six new Discovery Groups through this on-the-spot approach to building a relationship with strangers and to starting to read Bible stories with them.

You need to understand that this isn't just something that Jesus is doing in places like Iran and Afghanistan. He is doing it in the West as well, because this isn't man's idea. It is the wisdom of the Forgotten Manifesto of Jesus, and it can happen anytime, anywhere, with anyone.

8

Discovery Groups

Luke 10:7

"Stay there, eating and drinking whatever they give you, for the worker deserves his wages. Do not move around from house to house." (Luke 10:7)

Whenever the Seventy-Two received a warm welcome from people, Jesus commanded them to clear their schedules so that they could spend time with them. They were not to keep on moving, like rolling stones which gather no moss. They were to invest the time it takes to train people in what it means to follow Jesus. This is one of the great paradoxes of disciple-making movements. To reach a nation, we must narrow our attention to discipling a handful of people. To have a big impact, we must keep our focus small.

"To reach a nation, we must narrow our attention to discipling a handful of people."

Jesus modeled this for us when he "appointed twelve *that they might be with him* [my italics]" (Mark 3:14). Although he ministered to large crowds, he restricted his disciple-making focus to the few. Jesus was forever inviting himself into people's homes to eat and drink with them.[1] As he did so, he invited them to reflect with him on passages of Scripture to find answers to their questions in the Word of God. Jesus therefore commissions the Twelve and

---

1   Matthew 11:19; Luke 5:29–30, 19:5–10; John 1:38–39, 12:2.

Seventy-Two to do the same. He does not send them out as traveling rabbis to offer public lectures in theology. He sends them out in pairs to stay in people's houses, eating and drinking with them, showing them how to live as his disciples by embodying it for them in their homes.

The Seventy-Two were to do what they had seen Jesus do. After Jesus became a guest at the home of Zacchaeus, the tax collector announced to his neighbors that he would obey the scripture which commanded people to pay back four times whatever they had swindled from others. When Jesus found two potential dinner hosts in Emmaus, we are told that "beginning with Moses and all the Prophets, he explained to them what was said in all the Scriptures concerning himself." As a result, they marveled after dinner: "Were not our hearts burning within us while he ... opened the Scriptures to us?" Jesus taught his followers to make this the principal focus of their own ministry too. In the book of Acts, we find them moving in and out of people's homes, eating and drinking and studying passages of Scripture together, spurring one another on to obey Jesus fully.[2]

We have found that the best way for us to do this today is to help our People of Peace to begin "Discovery Groups" in their homes. If we are working with teenagers or adults who do not own their own home, we help them to create a similar setting in a local café or in their school canteen. *Where* a Discovery Group meets matters far less than why it meets: so that the Person of Peace can invite others to come on a journey of discovery with them.

"Eating and drinking" means that a Discovery Group should spend unhurried time hanging out with one another. Mealtimes are a perfect opportunity to do this, but the key here isn't food and drink. It is time. Making disciples cannot be accomplished through a weekly meeting on its own. When Jesus tells us in Luke 10:7 that

---

2 Luke 19:8 appears to have been prompted by Exodus 22:1 and 2 Samuel 12:6. See also Luke 24:27–32; Acts 18:26, 20:20; Hebrews 10:24–25.

"the worker deserves his wages," he is probably teaching us not to feel guilty about eating the food of our People of Peace, because it is a fair price for the mentoring we give them. But since the workers Jesus mentions in Luke 10:2 are the People of Peace, we could also read it to mean that we must not short-change them by being stingy toward them with our time. If we have found a Person of Peace, then they are worthy of our time and energy. Making disciples is like parenting: it doesn't happen unless we pour our lives into them. Even a full-time disciple-maker will find it difficult to mentor more than five Discovery Groups effectively at any one time, which is why we are so diligent about sifting whether or not we have met a true Person of Peace, because each one requires so much time.

> **"Making disciples is like parenting: it doesn't happen unless we pour our lives into them."**

If a Discovery Group only gathers for a weekly Bible study, then its interactions remain superficial, so the changes that the Holy Spirit makes in people's lives are likely to be shallow. If a Discovery Group is all about socializing and neglects deep study of the Scriptures, then people are unlikely to hear God speak to them. They will experience little of his power in their own lives, and they will have little motivation to share with others.

To make the most of our time together, we have therefore learned to use each gathering to ask seven simple questions of a Bible story. Our goal is to train people to stand on their own two feet as followers of Jesus, so each of these "7 Qs" seeks to impart one of the seven strands that we see in the spiritual DNA of any disciple of Jesus (see Figure 8.1). Asking the same seven questions each time makes it easy for the Person of Peace to become the group facilitator, and for the others in the group to learn to lead groups of their own. It takes about an hour for a group of five and two hours for a group of ten.

1 **What are we thankful for?**
DNA of Worship

2 **What are we struggling with?**
DNA of Prayer

3 **How can we help people with their struggles?**
DNA of Ministry

4 **How did we do with our action steps from last time?**
DNA of Accountability

Read / reread / retell the Bible story

5 **What does this teach us about God and about people?**
DNA of Discovery

6 **What do we feel led to change after reading this story?**
DNA of Obedience

7 **Who will we share with this week?**
DNA of Evangelism

Figure 8.1 The "7 Qs" – seven questions to ask in a Discovery Group discussion

The first two questions seek to impart to people the DNA of Worship and the DNA of Prayer. Since most groups consist of nonbelievers in the early days, we cannot expect them to know instinctively how to talk with God. By asking "What are we thankful for?" and "What are we struggling with?", we train them to speak out their praise and petitions to God. As they learn to articulate the highs and lows of their lives to other people, they naturally learn how to speak about those same things to God in heartfelt worship and prayer.

The third question seeks to impart to people the DNA of Ministry. It would be wrong for us to respond to people's honesty about their struggles by shrugging our shoulders and rushing into Bible study. We want to use this moment to help people to reflect on how God might want to use them to meet many of the needs that have just been shared. As a Discovery Group becomes established, we usually discover that a wider sense of ministry develops toward the needs of people who are outside the group. The question "How can we help people with their struggles?" becomes a stimulus for serving people in the wider community. That's often how many more People of Peace are found.

The fourth question seeks to impart to people the DNA of Accountability. Jesus insists that we are not blessed merely by hearing his Word, but by doing what it says.[3] The question "How did we do with our action steps from last time?" helps people to reflect on their obedience to what they felt the Lord was telling them to do in questions six and seven of the previous discussion. It fulfills the command in Hebrews 10:24–25 that we should gather together in order to "spur one another on toward love and good deeds."

Between the fourth and fifth questions, we invite people to read the next Bible story to continue their journey of discovery. Since

---

3   John 13:17. Both the wise and foolish builders hear the Word of God in Matthew 7:24–27. The difference between them is that only the wise builder "hears these words of mine and puts them into practice."

Scripture teaches us that faith comes by hearing God's Word and that we need help for God's Word to penetrate our hearts, we may ask two different people to read the story out loud a couple of times, and we may ask one or two others to retell it in their own words. The exact way we do this may vary, based on literacy levels and preferred styles of learning, but the key thing is that we never rush it. We do all we can to help people to digest God's Word slowly and carefully.[4]

The fifth question seeks to impart to people the DNA of Discovery. We resist the urge to offer people our own insights into the passage. We are the facilitators – the Holy Spirit is the teacher. Instead, we ask, "What does this teach us about God and about people?" – then, like Jesus in Matthew 16:13–20, we try to stand back and allow God's Spirit to bring revelation to people directly through God's Word. Doing this also enables the Person of Peace to emerge as the group facilitator instead of us, since anybody, even a nonbeliever, can ask the same simple question of any Bible story.

"We are the facilitators – the Holy Spirit is the teacher."

The sixth question seeks to impart the DNA of Obedience. The question "What do we feel led to change after reading this story?" is vital, because the extent to which each member of the Discovery Group will experience God at work in their lives is the extent to which they are willing to obey him. We always let each person set their own action steps, because we don't want people to obey us. We want to coach them to obey what they sense God is saying to them. During the first few weeks, when the group mainly consists of nonbelievers, we may need to rephrase this question as, "If what we just read together is true, what would we need to change?", but as time goes on it becomes natural for them to consider how they

---

4   Romans 10:17; Luke 8:11–12.

should obey what God is saying to them.[5] Obedience to God is what leads to experiencing God, and experiencing God is what leads to sharing with others.

The seventh question seeks to impart the DNA of Evangelism. "Who will we share with this week?" is not an encouragement for people to rush out to tell their friends and family all about Jesus. Like us, they need to go slow to go fast, so we quickly train them in the "7 Ss" of how to share. We assume that everybody in the Discovery Group wants to obey God and to share what they are learning with others, so we touch base with each of them throughout the week to help them troubleshoot any problems they are having with their obedience and evangelism goals. It is as they obey God through their answers to these last two questions that they begin to experience God and come to faith in him.

You won't find these seven questions listed in Luke 10, but we think they represent the type of questions that the Seventy-Two asked their People of Peace as they ate and drank together in their homes. These questions echo how Jesus and the early Christians interact with people in the gospels and the book of Acts. As we have learned to use these "7 Qs," we have found that they have helped us to make strong disciples of Jesus everywhere.

The process is simple. The textbook is God's Word. The teacher is God's Spirit. The priority is obedience and sharing with others. The result is a disciple-making movement.

---

5   This is an important distinction. When church leaders insist that people obey *them*, it leads to legalism and manipulation. When church leaders help people to hear and obey *God*, it leads to life and freedom.

Saudi Arabia: Mathieson's story

My wife and I never expected it to be easy as Western missionaries to Saudi Arabia. But nor did we expect it to be this hard. People seemed so resistant when we tried to share Jesus with them.

Our discouragement lifted briefly when a friend in the West managed to link us up with a small group of Christians in our city. Our hearts soared to hear Saudis worshiping the Lord in their own language. This was the dream that had brought us here! But after a few months, our discouragement returned. We didn't feel that we were getting anywhere with these believers. They had been trained to expect white Westerners to lead everything for them. No matter how much we spoon-fed them from the Bible, they showed no signs of maturing into leadership or of developing any appetite to share the good news about Jesus with Saudi Muslims. This made us more discouraged than ever. We felt like we were banging our heads against a brick wall.

The Lord must have seen how much we were struggling, because he mercifully provided us with a mentor. Through the friend of a friend of a friend, we were able to connect with one of the Iranian house-church leaders via a video call. We immediately hit it off with him. The fact that he started by coaching us to pray and fast for breakthrough set our hearts at ease. It was clear that he wanted to help us to develop our relationship with God, not just our missionary methodology. His focus on radical obedience to the Scriptures was also refreshing. We felt that at last we had found someone who knew how to help us.

Sadly, not everyone in our small group of believers felt the same way. A few were offended by the directness of our Iranian brother's teaching. Although it broke my heart to see them drop out of our regular coaching calls, those who remained began developing a real faith and hunger to make disciples across Saudi Arabia. They were eager to go out on the streets together, which made my wife and me feel nervous, but we were out of any other answers! We resolved that we would do what the Iranians taught us. We would follow the Forgotten Manifesto of Jesus, come what may.

My natural instinct was to take a lead, but we decided to do what Luke 10 teaches us by putting the Saudi believers front and center in our outreach. I adopted a coaching role in the background, helping these "insiders" to go out in pairs onto the streets and into stores in search of People of Peace. We instinctively wanted to focus our efforts on the affluent parts of our city, where most of us lived and where we were likely to meet well-educated and well-connected Saudis. However, our Iranian coaches insisted we must go to the poorest parts of the city, where we felt most out of our depth and most dependent on God. This was also where we were most likely to find "little people."

It took us about a year before we started to see breakthrough. That's how long it took us to learn the art of striking up fruitful gospel conversations. We had to learn to start with **simple** (usually a conversation starter around family or football) and then to deepen our conversations and become more **serious**, then **spiritual**. We had to learn how to be honest about our own lives in order to make people feel comfortable reciprocating by sharing their own **struggles** with us. Operating in a country where attempting to convert a Muslim can be punished with imprisonment, or even execution, we were particularly keen to learn how to **sift** people to verify if they were truly hungry to receive our message.

If they were, we began to share **stories** from the Bible with them and we prayed for them to have a **supernatural**

encounter with God. It took us about a year to perfect these new skills, but as we persevered we began to flush out People of Peace, searching for faith in Jesus even at the epicenter of Islam.

We have been doing this now for two years. It still feels like early days for us, but we are excited about some of the progress that we are making. We have learned to pray less for ourselves and more for the Lord to lead us to more laborers in the harvest field, since it is a focus on finding People of Peace which seems to stimulate disciple-making movements. We find that roughly one out of every four people we meet is willing to open up to us about their struggles. One in four of those is willing to read Bible stories with us. One in four of those shares with their friends and family and starts a Discovery Group in their home. That's a fourth of a fourth of a fourth – or one in every sixty-four people we talk to. It's a lot of hard work to find a genuine Person of Peace, but it is worth it for the rapid advances we see whenever we do. Let me give you a couple of real-life examples.

One of our team met Abdullah and took the conversation from simple to serious. When he asked Abdullah, "What struggles are you and your family facing right now?", Abdullah opened up about his failure to control his anger and how he knew that it was ruining his family. Our team member asked if he would like some help with this. He had some stories from the Prophets which might serve as an effective anger-management course for him. When Abdullah invited our team member into his home to read the stories together, he met Abdullah's wife and children. He also learned about Abdullah's depression and the further damage that this was causing to his family. They formed a Discovery Group together thirteen weeks ago – and here's where it gets really exciting. Abdullah introduced our team member to four of his friends so that they could discuss the Bible stories together. One of those friends introduced Abdullah to a larger group of twenty-five friends who were interested too. Our team member is now training up Abdullah to lead new Discovery Groups for several of those Saudi friends.

A second example is Ibrahim, the imam of a mosque in one of the suburbs of our city. Because we have taken him slowly and respectfully through the Bible stories, he has begun to share them with his congregation. He recently began a Discovery Group in the gardens of his mosque for some of its members who are interested in finding out more.

Abdullah and Ibrahim are both still Muslims. Neither has come through yet to sufficient faith in Jesus for us to baptize him as a born-again believer. Nevertheless, they are happy for us to continue meeting up with them and discipling them through the Christian Scriptures, and they have become our fellow workers in the harvest field. We are not impatient that it is taking them a few months to understand and respond to the gospel through our Bible studies. You can't expect to see fruit overnight when you are working with the Muslims of Saudi Arabia! Nevertheless, after less than two years, we now have sixteen Discovery Groups gathering Muslims in houses right across our city. All of those groups are led by Muslims whom we are discipling toward faith in Jesus and who are being coached by us in how to lead great Bible discussions. We are confident that out of these groups will emerge many other groups like them.

I want to commend you for reading this book and for taking seriously the instructions of Jesus in Luke 10. Most of our breakthroughs in Saudi Arabia can be traced back to our decision to learn from our Iranian brothers and sisters that these verses are the Forgotten Manifesto of Jesus.

One last example: On a recent trip to one of the poorest areas of our city, I felt the Lord challenge me about the cell phone and the credit card that I was carrying in my pocket. I felt him remind me of his command to take no purse or moneybag, so I resolved to act as if I didn't have them with me. This meant asking a Pakistani taxi driver if he would help me out, as I had no way of getting home. This prompted a great conversation between us, which resulted in him inviting me into his home and introducing me to fifty leading members of the Pakistani community in our city!

Now I regularly leave my cell phone and my credit card at home. By deliberately placing myself in need, I find that I am able to connect more easily with potential People of Peace. I want to encourage you to think about how you might do the same thing where you are.

What you are learning through this book is much more than a method. It is a manifesto from Jesus, which teaches us how to pursue the Great Commission in a new way – in God's way.

9

Multiplying House Churches

Luke 10:7

"Stay there, eating and drinking whatever they give you, for the worker deserves his wages. Do not move around from house to house." (Luke 10:7)

In 2008, three former roommates from San Francisco launched a quiet revolution. They created the website *airbnb.com* to empower ordinary people to rent out their spare bedrooms like a hotel. You probably know the rest of the story. Within a short space of time, Airbnb was offering more rooms for rent than the world's top five hotel chains put together. Within ten years, Airbnb had become a $30 billion company.

Jesus launches a similar but far greater revolution as he sends the Seventy-Two into the towns and villages of Israel. Up until this moment, everyone has thought about religion in terms of sacred buildings. The Jews have built a beautiful Temple in Jerusalem, supplemented by synagogue buildings in their other towns. The pagans have built their own sacred temples too. Everyone agrees that the proper place for people to practice religion is in a custom-made religious building.

Jesus upends this when he commands the Seventy-Two to center their ministry in people's homes. He doesn't tell them to create a network of Christian synagogue buildings. That would require far too much money and time. It would also divert their focus from the harvest fields. We shape our buildings and then they shape us, so Jesus tells the Seventy-Two to dispense with buildings altogether.

Jesus tells one of his People of Peace why: "A time is coming when you will worship the Father neither on this mountain nor in Jerusalem ... A time is coming and has now come when the true worshipers will worship the Father in the Spirit and in truth, for they are the kind of worshipers the Father seeks" (John 4:21–23). Jesus wants us to grasp that God's plan for the world is about sacred people, not about sacred buildings.

> **"We shape our buildings and then they shape us, so Jesus tells the Seventy-Two to dispense with buildings altogether."**

The gospel has spread rapidly across Iran over the past few years because the Iranian believers have wholeheartedly embraced this key aspect of the Forgotten Manifesto of Jesus. You must understand that they do not own any buildings. They do not have a website or any Western-style church structure.[1] They have done what Jesus commanded and unleashed the latent power of people's homes to reach their nation. Once most of the people in a Discovery Group have become baptized believers, they recognize it as a house church. What we were forced to do in Iran due to persecution, we now do all over the world gladly, because it is what Jesus has commanded his followers to do.

Jesus preached in the Jewish synagogues, but he tended to see most of his fruit when he left sacred spaces behind to teach and heal in people's homes. Don't miss the significance, therefore, when he does not send the Seventy-Two to seek out synagogue services, and in the book of Acts when the early Christians reach Jerusalem from an upper room, from the house of Mary and from the homes of countless unnamed, ordinary believers. Peter reaches

---

1 Nor do any of their house churches have a name. They are simply "the church at so-and-so's house" – rather like the churches in Romans 16:5, 1 Corinthians 16:19, Colossians 4:15 and Philemon 2.

Caesarea from the home of Cornelius. Paul reaches Philippi from the homes of Lydia and the local jailer. He reaches Thessalonica and Corinth from the houses of Jason, Priscilla and Aquila, Titius Justus and Stephanas. He reaches Troas from a humble third-story apartment. He reaches Ephesus from the houses of unnamed believers. He reaches Colossae from the house of Philemon, Apphia and Archippus. He reaches Rome from his own rental home.[2] The early Christians seek out People of Peace by chatting to them in the Temple courtyards and the lecture hall of Tyrannus, since those are busy public spaces, but they don't try to set up churches there. For them, it was always home sweet home.

In his seminal history of the early church, Michael Green reflects:

> The "church in the house" became a crucial factor in the spread of the Christian faith ... Christian missionaries made a deliberate point of gaining whatever households they could as lighthouses, so to speak, from which the gospel could illuminate the surrounding darkness ... [We must not underestimate] the centrality of the household to Christian advance.[3]

When the emperor Constantine declared himself to be a Christian at the start of the fourth century, the Church's rapid growth began to stall. The focus shifted away from gathering together in homes toward gathering in sacred buildings, and from ordinary leaders toward professionals. Many of the revival movements that have rejuvenated the Church in the days since Constantine have done so by restoring the Church to its former setting in the home. The medieval monks withdrew from sacred buildings to form their own communities in private dwellings. The radical reformers

---

2 Acts 1:13, 2:46, 5:42, 10:24–27, 12:12, 16:15, 16:32–34, 17:5, 18:7, 18:26, 20:7–9, 20:20, 28:30–31; Romans 16:3–5; 1 Corinthians 16:19; Philemon 1–2.

3 Michael Green, *Evangelism in the Early Church* (London: Hodder & Stoughton, 1970).

accused Martin Luther and John Calvin of being "halfway men" for reforming the Church's doctrine but never challenging its fundamental form. John and Charles Wesley were both converted through Bible study groups in the houses of their friends. Although the Methodist revival is most famous for seeking out converts through open-air preaching, the backbone of their disciple-making movement was the class meetings which the Wesleys established in people's homes. In recent years, the gospel has spread rapidly throughout China and India and Indonesia and Iran through similar movements of house churches.

As *Sheep Among Wolves*, we therefore take this strategy of Jesus very seriously. We believe he meant it when he instructed the Seventy-Two: "When you enter a house ... stay there." Our goal is to help every Discovery Group to mature into a Multiplying House Church – not just a traditional church service relocated to a home, but a miniature mission station. If the majority of members come to faith in Jesus quickly, then it is not unusual for us to recognize a Person of Peace as the leader of a Multiplying House Church within a few months of our discovering them. If this feels fast to people who have grown up with more traditional church structures, then note that it is what Paul and Barnabas did on their missionary journeys. Only a few months after finding People of Peace in the major towns of southern Turkey, "Paul and Barnabas appointed elders for them in each church and, with prayer and fasting, committed them to the Lord, in whom they had put their trust" (Acts 14:23).[4]

We expect all of our house churches to be **self-governing**, since our experience is that centralized control stifles movement.[5] We

---

4 This is not the place for us to discuss the detail of church government. We do this as part of our coaching calls. In brief, we want the members of a house church to be able to read the New Testament and know from their experience what Bible words such as "church" and "elder" and "deacon" and "apostle" ought to mean.

5 Our house churches are nothing like the midweek cell groups that can be found in Western churches. A cell group is a subdivision of a centralized church structure, which sets their direction, baptizes their converts and manages their money. Our house churches are autonomous churches in every biblical sense of the word.

expect them to be **self-funding**, which isn't hard because small groups of Christians meeting in homes rarely require paid pastors. Everyone is trained from day one to start a new Discovery Group of their own, so our house churches never remain too large for too long. Our experience is that paying pastors is a movement killer. Human nature means that people are reluctant to do for free what they see others being paid to do. Money must not create a clergy/laity divide.

We expect all of our house churches to be **self-correcting**. Our experience is that when "outsiders" tell local believers what it ought to mean for them to live as Christians in their culture, it tends to lead to superficial changes and to legalism. Much deeper change comes when "insiders," who are more familiar with the local culture, are empowered to work out how to "take captive every thought to make it obedient to Christ" (2 Corinthians 10:5).

We expect all our house churches to be **self-replicating**. We do not have a centralized strategy for how we will make disciples across the world, any more than we did in the early days across Iran. All we ask is that each church follows the Forgotten Manifesto of Jesus. We know that if every house church prays for God to lead them to People of Peace in new areas, and if they help those People of Peace to take their friends on a journey of discovery, then the Church as a whole will succeed in making disciples of all nations.

This aspect of the Forgotten Manifesto is probably hardest to accept for Christians in Europe and North America, who have many centuries of church tradition to unravel. But ask yourself this question: What was Jesus trying to teach his Church in Europe and North America through the COVID-19 lockdown? What do you think he was trying to say to Western Christians during the many months that their church buildings were closed?

"What was Jesus trying to teach his Church in Europe and North America through the COVID-19 lockdown?"

Was he alerting them to the fatal passivity that we foster whenever we equate discipleship with sitting in rows and listening to gifted people on a platform? Was he trying to bring them back to more interactive gatherings, in which they could offer genuine mutual accountability to one another? Was he trying to show them a way in which the gospel could spread rapidly across the post-Christian landscape of Europe and North America?

In the West as much as in the East, houses remain the basic building blocks of society. That's why they still remain at the heart of God's strategy to reach the world.

Turkey: Andrew and Eleanor's story

We were born in England, but we have served as missionaries to Turkey for over twenty years. It didn't take us very long to fall in love with the Turkish people, but it has taken us more than two decades to understand how the Lord wants to train us to reach them.

We have spent the bulk of our time here attempting to start churches along the same lines as the churches we grew up in back at home. It was a real wake-up call for us to look around one day at the people in our church and to realize that as many Turks had left us through the back door as had joined us through the front door. Our church growth had come mainly from attracting expats and refugees, not Turkish people. This was not the only unpalatable truth that we needed to face up to at that time. Our church was still led by foreigners and dependent on foreign money to survive, which had created an unhealthy culture of dependency and a lot of pastoral issues across the church.

We reached out to one of our friends to express some of these concerns. Our friend disarmed us by responding simply: "Then you need to start discipling the Turkish believers." Although this is such a central theme of the New Testament, it seemed revolutionary to us. It started us out on a journey toward discovering what it means for us to "go and make disciples."

We first met the Iranian leaders when one of them spoke at a missionary conference we attended. Gradually, because of this and our own Bible study, the direction of our ministry began to change. We started going out in search of People of Peace and then discipling them through a discovery process rather than through sermons or traditional Bible studies. Since Jesus tells us to ask our People of Peace to provide the venue, gather the people, and serve the food and drink to them, we began to expect the Turks to take a lead. This was the exact opposite of what we had been doing through our attractional model of Sunday church.

It has taken us five years to learn this new model of ministry. We had so much to "deprogram" from our former lives. At first, we tried to combine what we were learning from Luke 10 with our traditional Sunday morning church. Our attempts to create a hybrid model failed pretty badly! We needed to face up to the fact that God was calling us to pursue something entirely new – or something old, since it is really a case of going back to the gospels and the book of Acts. We left our church and started again from scratch, with just our family and two Turkish believers. It was difficult, but it was only after this that things began to get exciting!

One of the two Turkish believers was a man named Yusuf. We baptized him as a follower of Jesus and prayed for him to be filled with the Holy Spirit. We spent a lot of time with him, helping him to learn how to obey Jesus amid some of the problems that he was facing with his family. Both of us saw him as a very unlikely leader, but we were learning to trust the Lord for "little people." It is through Yusuf that our tiny house church began to multiply rapidly.

Yusuf lived in a different part of Istanbul from us, so one day when I traveled to see him I deliberately provoked him: "Wouldn't it be great if we could start another group like ours in this area?" A couple of weeks later, while he was reading his Bible in a local café, two Turkish men struck up a conversation with him. They were baptized believers but they had dropped out of church. Yusuf quickly invited them to meet with him to read some Bible stories together. Very soon, he found himself leading a Discovery Group for them and half a dozen of their friends.

I thank God that he gave me the wisdom to back off a little when this happened. Instead of joining Yusuf's group so that I could help him, I took a step back and assumed the role of coach. I regularly met up with Yusuf to help him grow as a leader, but I allowed him to lead the group on his own. I invested some of the time that this saved into concerted prayer for Yusuf and the people in his group. I believe this was key to turning his Discovery Group into a disciple-making movement.

Yusuf had a friend from the southeast of Turkey who was studying at university in Istanbul. Although he was from a Muslim background and not interested himself, he told Yusuf that many of his friends back home were asking questions about God. Yusuf decided to take a trip to the southeast of Turkey and, in his own words, spent ten days talking with those friends about God from morning till night. After he left, one of them continued the discussions under Yusuf's guidance. That initial Discovery Group has now launched eight more groups in that southeastern city, plus a further seven in two other cities!

Yusuf's method of starting groups is really simple: he befriends a person who introduces him to their group of friends, then he casts a vision for them to begin a Discovery Group together. He has recently started two new groups this way in Istanbul – one for a group of girls through a girl who works in his father's shop, and one for a group of guys through a man he met outside the shop.

We still feel that we are in the early days of our disciple-making movement. I don't want to pretend that we are seeing anything close yet to what our friends are seeing in Iran. However, when we returned to Istanbul a few weeks ago after two months on furlough in England, we discovered that six more Discovery Groups had started in our absence. Twenty-five people in the existing groups had also been baptized. Nineteen of the Discovery Groups have now transitioned into house churches, and some of the groups that they have started are now starting new groups of their own. The People of Peace we found are now finding their own People of Peace, who are also finding further People of Peace! That's three generations of disciples. We are so grateful to God, and we believe that this is only the beginning.

We shared our story with many people during a recent trip to England. Some of them responded, "This is all very well in Turkey, but it would never work in Western Europe." We found this interesting, because many of the Turkish leaders tell us that they think Luke 10 will work in the West but it won't work where they are. People have the same faith struggles everywhere!

Jesus promises us that "The harvest is plentiful, but the workers are few." Whether in the East or in the West, God is preparing a harvest of people who are hungry to know and experience him. Luke 10 gives us universal principles for disciple-making everywhere.

If it feels daunting for you to believe that the Lord will help you to see similar breakthroughs where you are, be encouraged. Our God loves to work in the hardest places!

10

Creation to Christ

Luke 10:8–9

"Heal the sick who are there and tell them, 'The kingdom of God has come near to you.'" (Luke 10:9)

There is a world of difference between telling people what to think and leading them on a journey of discovery. The first produces students who are dependent on you as their teacher. They learn at a shallow level, expecting you to do their thinking for them. When a more gifted teacher comes along, what they believe changes with their teacher. The second is what leads to the deep work of disciple-making. Leading people on a journey of discovery makes room for the Holy Spirit to become people's teacher. It encourages them to think for themselves and to become active leaders in God's ever-growing gospel team of harvest workers. It lies at the heart of the Forgotten Manifesto of Jesus.

We take the model for our Discovery Groups from the way that Jesus mentored two of his followers in Luke 24:13–35. Jesus has just been raised from the dead when he finds two confused and crestfallen friends walking and talking together on the road from Jerusalem to Emmaus. You might want to turn to that passage as you read this chapter, because it reveals how Jesus wants us to take people on a journey of discovery.

The first thing that Jesus does is to conceal his identity from his two followers. This is so surprising that the passage says it twice. "They were kept from recognizing him" (verse 16) until "their eyes were opened and they recognized him" (verse 31). Many people find this confusing. Jesus is in the perfect position to brush away their struggle in a moment. All he needs to do is show them the nail marks in his hands and feet, and they will instantly believe. Yet this is not what Jesus does. He doesn't wow them with a miracle because he does not want their faith in him to remain superficial. Instead, he conceals the truth from them so that he can take them through a number of Old Testament stories. He knows that if he gives them instant answers to their questions, their conversion will be joyful but shallow, so he resolves to go slow to go fast with them. "Beginning with Moses and all the Prophets, he explained to them what was said in all the Scriptures concerning himself" (verse 27).

> ## "The first thing that Jesus does is to conceal his identity from his two followers."

Jesus starts with **simple**. He greets the two friends and gently falls in beside them as they walk along the road. When the time is right, he becomes **serious**. He asks them questions which invite them to open up about why their faces look so sad. Because Jesus takes things at the right pace, they are happy for the conversation to become **spiritual** and to open up to him about their **struggle**. They share their confusion that Jesus of Nazareth, who they hoped was the Messiah, has recently been crucified by his enemies. Their last ray of hope had been that Jesus predicted he would die and come back from the dead three days later, but it is now Sunday evening. The three-day deadline has expired on that hope too. Some of their female friends claim to have seen Jesus raised back to life, but none of the apostles can corroborate that story. The two men confess freely to the stranger on the road to Emmaus that they are struggling to know who or what to believe.

This feels like another perfect moment for Jesus to reveal his identity to them. He can clear up their confusion in a moment, yet his goal is something greater. He wants to help these two friends to become real disciples, and for that he needs to take them on a journey of discovery through several Scripture **stories**. He must make room for the Holy Spirit to teach them what the Word of God says about their struggle. Starting with the first five books of the Old Testament, which were written by Moses, he therefore leads them through the Prophets and the other Jewish Scriptures.[1] It is seven miles from Jerusalem to Emmaus, so Jesus has two to three hours in which to take them from Creation to Christ.

Miracles tend to persuade people for a moment, whereas Discovery Bible Study imparts faith which lasts a lifetime. Jesus pretends to be traveling on beyond Emmaus in order to **sift** whether the two friends want to engage further with his Scripture stories. It is only when they invite him to stay the night at their home that he finally performs a miracle to confirm that the message of his Scripture stories is true. Jesus grants them a **supernatural encounter** to confirm their discovery process, not to do away with their need for it. When the two friends witness Jesus disappearing before their eyes, they are persuaded that God's Spirit has indeed been speaking to them through God's Word. "Were not our hearts burning within us while he talked with us on the road and opened the Scriptures to us?"(verse 32). It is late in the day and Jerusalem is seven miles away, but nothing can stop them from hurrying back to share the truth they have discovered about Jesus with all of their friends.

> **"Miracles tend to persuade people for a moment, whereas Discovery Bible Study imparts faith which lasts a lifetime."**

I hope that this brief study of Luke 24 persuades you that the "7 Ss" are more than merely our own clever thinking (see Figure 10.1). This is how Jesus shared the good news of the gospel with people. If even Jesus needed to be patient and to take people on a journey

---

1 The books of the Old Testament appear in the Jewish Scriptures in a different order from ours. They are divided into Torah, Prophets and Writings, which Luke summarizes as "Moses ... the Prophets ... all the Scriptures" (verse 27).

of discovery, then how could we ever imagine that we are able to shortcut the process? If Jesus was careful to go slow to go fast with people, then how much more must we learn to do so?

SIMPLE

SERIOUS

SPIRITUAL

STRUGGLE

SIFT

STORIES

SUPERNATURAL ENCOUNTER

Figure 10.1 The "7 Ss" – seven stages in a go-slow-to-go-fast gospel conversation

We have learned to imitate Jesus in Luke 24 by helping our People of Peace to read a series of Bible stories that take them from **Creation to Christ** (see Figure 10.2).[2] We avoid using religious terms, such as

---

2   For a list of which truths we expect people to discover through each of these stories, see Appendix, pages 193–94.

1   **Genesis 1:1 – 2:3** – God creates the world

2   **Genesis 2:4–25** – God creates man and woman

3   **Genesis 3:1–13** – Man and woman disobey God

4   **Genesis 3:14–24** – God judges a sinful world

5   **Genesis 6:5 – 7:24** – God destroys evil humanity

6   **Genesis 8:1 – 9:17** – God's covenant with Noah

7   **Genesis 12:1–8, 15:1–6, 17:1–7** – God's covenant with Abraham

8   **Genesis 22:1–19** – Abraham gives his son as an offering

9   **Exodus 12:1–28** – The promise of Passover

10 **Exodus 20:1–21** – The Ten Commandments

11 **Leviticus 4:1–35** – The sin offering

12 **Isaiah 53:1–12** – The promise of a better way

13 **Luke 1:26–38, 2:1–20** – The birth of Jesus

14 **Matthew 3:1–17; John 1:29–34** – Jesus is baptized

15 **Matthew 4:1–11** – Jesus is tested

16 **John 3:1–21** – Jesus and Nicodemus

17 **John 4:1–26, 39–42** – Jesus and the woman at the well

18 **Luke 5:17–26** – Jesus heals the paralyzed man

19 **Mark 4:35–41** – Jesus calms the storm

20 **Mark 5:1–20** – Jesus casts out evil spirits

21 **John 11:1–44** – Jesus raises a man from the dead

22 **Matthew 26:17–30** – Jesus predicts his betrayal and the New Covenant

23 **John 18:1 – 19:16** – Jesus is betrayed and condemned

24 **Luke 23:32–56** – Jesus is crucified

25 **Luke 24:1–35** – Jesus conquers death

26 **Luke 24:36–53** – Jesus appears and ascends

27 **John 3:1–21** – We have a choice to make

Figure 10.2 **Creation to Christ stories – 27 key passages**

"church" or "Christian" or "Christ," until the stories introduce those words to people. Jesus warns us in John 6:44–45 that the Holy Spirit alone can reveal spiritual truth to people, so we take care not to run ahead of his work in people's hearts. Whenever we do so, we always regret it, because it provokes people to pull their spiritual shutters down.[3]

When people see this long list of twenty-seven Bible stories, they often raise the objection that helping people through this discovery process would take them far too long. They have not yet grasped that our goal is far bigger than persuading people to pray a sinner's prayer with us. We want to teach them how to live the rest of their lives as disciples of Jesus. Imparting the DNA of discipleship to people is a process that takes time! Whenever we have looked for shortcuts, it has always proven to be a false economy.

> ### "Imparting the DNA of discipleship to people is a process that takes time!"

Then there are others who are happy to take people through these twenty-seven stories, but they want to do it at breakneck speed. The idea of leading people through a discovery process over twenty-seven weeks feels far too slow to them. They have not yet fully grasped that our goal is to give the Holy Spirit time to speak to people through God's Word. In the Parable of the Sower, in Luke 8:4–15, Jesus warns us that it takes time for Scripture to penetrate the hard ground of people's hearts. Even after it does so, it takes time for them to develop deep roots of discipleship that will sustain their faith in God through the ups and downs of following Jesus for the long haul. It takes time for the Scriptures to root out the vicious

---

3 Yes, Acts 17:18 summarizes Paul's message to the pagans as "Jesus and the resurrection," but Acts 14:14–17 and 17:22–31 clarify what he actually said. He was careful not to speak words such as "Jesus" or "Bible" prematurely. We have to help the faster learners in our Discovery Groups to grasp this principle. If one group member receives revelation from the Holy Spirit earlier than the others, then we do what Jesus did. We take them aside and we warn them not to tell the others what they have seen until the Holy Spirit also reveals it to them.

thorns of their old way of living that will strangle the life out of their new relationship with God. We have learned to take people slowly through this discovery process because we believe that this is what helps People of Peace to yield fruit thirty, sixty or a hundred times what we are able to sow into their hearts.

Our ultimate goal in this is the same as that of Jesus on the road to Emmaus. He wasn't just engaging in personal evangelism. He was introducing his companions to a discovery process that they could hurry back and share with their friends in Jerusalem. Remember, our definition of a Person of Peace is "a nonbeliever who is willing to gather a group of nonbelievers to go on a journey of discovery with them." We don't skip over any of the stories if a Person of Peace already knows them, since our goal is to help them use the stories to make disciples of their family and friends.[4] We use the same set of stories with everyone, and we ask the same seven questions of each story, because we want every group member to be able to replicate the process with anybody, anywhere.[5] One of the reasons why disciple-making movements reach such large numbers of people is that the process is easy to replicate. We don't need to run separate training courses to teach people how to start new Discovery Groups. They simply do for others what has been done for them.[6]

So, let's learn from Jesus on the road to Emmaus. Instead of blurting out too quickly what we think people ought to believe, let's give the Holy Spirit enough time to reveal truth to them and to impart the DNA of discipleship to them. Let's patiently guide them on a journey of discovery through the Scriptures, from Creation to Christ.

4 We do not intend to remain part of the Discovery Group past Story 10. Instead, we deliberately foster insider ministry by coaching the Person of Peace to facilitate the group discussions without us.

5 For this reason, we avoid introducing outside materials into our Discovery Bible Studies. They might be great, but they make things less replicable. Using the same simple Bible stories means that anyone can lead.

6 In the first three weeks, we encourage people to invite their friends to join the group. After that, we encourage them to start new groups for their friends instead. *Adding people* transitions into *multiplying groups*.

Iraq: Hussein and Laila's story

As a teenager, I [Laila] began attending the local church youth group. My parents were furious when I told them I had decided to become a follower of Jesus. Hussein was intrigued, however, and began attending the youth group with me. When he gave his life to Jesus, the youth leader prophesied over him: "You will one day go back to Iraq and baptize many new believers." That prophetic word never left him, even when his devout Muslim mother banned him from attending church for several years.

After we were married, we became part of our British church leadership team. Hussein secured a top job at a computer consultancy. We became parents to three beautiful children. To those around us, it looked as if our lives were pretty perfect, but we couldn't shake off the feeling that the Lord was calling us to go back to our old city in Iraq. We discussed this sense of calling with our fellow church leaders, and they encouraged us to step out in obedience to the Lord. Just three months later, we moved our family back to the city that we had left behind as children.

"Why did you come back?" was the most common question that people asked us. Many Iraqis dream of emigrating to begin a new life in America or Europe, so it intrigued people that we had made the journey in the opposite direction! This gave us brilliant opportunities to speak to people about our faith in Jesus, but looking back we didn't really know how to share effectively with them. We built lots of great relationships with Western expat Christians and with the Iraqis who had joined their churches, but when Hussein was offered a job on the leadership team of one of those churches we began to reflect on whether we were achieving what we had moved back for. We were horrified when we made a sober assessment of our fruitfulness together. In two years, we hadn't managed to lead even one Iraqi to faith in Jesus.

The Lord was very good to us. He must have heard our troubled conversations, because at our lowest point we were introduced to the Iranian believers by a mutual friend. They offered to spend three whole days on a video call with us in order to explain the Forgotten Manifesto of Jesus to us from Luke 10. We would like to tell you that we instantly warmed to what they said to us, but that wouldn't be true. We were offended by three things that they said to us.

1 Don't begin by talking to people about Jesus, church or the Bible.
2 Don't introduce Jesus to people until Jesus begins to introduce himself.
3 Expect unbelievers to lead other unbelievers to faith in Jesus.

When we heard these three things, we both looked at each other. We had been married long enough to be able to read each other's minds. I [Laila] was most offended by the first two statements. I loved to speak about Jesus to people. It was why we moved back to Iraq! It felt like heresy for me to be told to hold back from proclaiming the name of Jesus to people. Hussein was more offended by the third statement. He had been responsible for pastoral care at our church back in England. He had witnessed people who had been Christians for many years struggling to live as disciples of Jesus. What the Iranians were suggesting sounded like the blind leading the blind! We thanked them for investing the three days with us, but we gave them a firm goodbye at the end.

At some point, however, during our third year back in Iraq, we finally hit the wall. We felt so depressed by our lack of fruitfulness that we began to reconsider what the Iranians had taught us. We patted ourselves on the back whenever we were able to speak the name of Jesus to people, but those three days of online training had helped us to see that our approach was alienating people. In our region of Iraq, the legal penalty for seeking to convert a Muslim to Christ is to be stoned to death. The people we spoke to about Jesus didn't try to stone us, but we realized that they were starting to avoid us. It was humbling to admit this, but we knew we needed help, so we reached out to the Iranians and asked if we could arrange another video call.

"Why did you bother to move back to Iraq?" We were a little taken aback by the Persian bluntness of their question. "Because we wanted to see our country turn to Jesus Christ as Lord." "Then why are you trying to plant a church instead of trying to start a movement of house churches?" Sensing our confusion, they patiently took us back over what they had tried to teach us from Luke 10.

We needed to learn to become more ambiguous. We stopped attending expat churches so that people would no longer pigeon-hole us as outsiders. We began to pray for God to lead us to People of Peace, and we went out into some of the poorest parts of our city to find them. Instead of trying to force-fit the name of Jesus into every conversation, we began to focus simply on loving people. We tried hard to unlearn our old habits and just to be friendly. We worked hard to learn the names of all the people we met and to ensure that they learned ours. Now when we walk through the bazaars and shopping malls of our Iraqi city, people run out of their shops to greet us. In all we do, we seek to follow the Forgotten Manifesto of Jesus.

We decided to pique people's curiosity. When they asked us, "Are you Muslims or Christians?", we began to reply: "Why do you think a person has to choose? We have a personal relationship with God – do you?" We began to ask five questions for every question that we answered. It seemed so counter-intuitive to us, but we were eager to learn from the wisdom of Jesus. And by God's grace, we started to see some small breakthroughs.

Hussein felt the Lord calling him to go to the red-light district of our city, where the streets are filled with drug addicts, alcoholics and male and female prostitutes. Seeing two men sitting in the gutter, he felt God prompt him to buy three sandwiches and to ask if he could share lunch with them. He was dressed plainly and had left his phone and credit cards behind, so they were happy to accept him as one of their own. Sadly, one of the men died two days later of liver failure, but before he died he introduced Hussein to his wider group of friends. Those friends went on to introduce Hussein to many of the other people in the red-light district. By going back to the same place consistently over time, we have now built many friendships as a family throughout that community. With some people, the conversation is still simple. With others, we have gone more serious. A surprising number of them have opened up to us about their struggles. We never try to share our stories from the Bible with people without first sense-checking whether or not they are open and hungry to learn. Unless we do so, we always find it is unfruitful even to try – people never stick with our Bible stories unless they count the cost up front and are clear about their struggle.

One couple were engaged to be married. As they got to know us over time, they commented that "We want to have what you both have together." We told them openly that "It is all down to our faith in God. We have a real relationship with him and we developed it through reading a collection of stories. Would you like to read them with us?" We read the first few stories with them and they were very open. Then, all of a sudden, things shut down. We discovered later that she was more interested in developing a relationship with God than he was. We have therefore put reading the stories with them on hold for a while. We still spend time with them, but we know that we can only move as quickly as the Holy Spirit is moving in their hearts. We are prepared to wait for them and for the others in their community. We will pick back up with them when they are ready.

Meanwhile, we were invited to drive for five hours to meet with a couple who lived in a remote village. They had expressed to a mutual friend of ours their desire for a real relationship with God. The friend responded that they needed to speak with us. When we got to their home after our long drive, we simply did what the Iranians taught us to do. We led them through a Discovery Bible Study, starting with Genesis 1. We began with our usual questions: "What are you both thankful for?" "What are you both struggling with right now?" Then we asked them to read the account of God creating the world. We asked them to retell the story in their own words, and then we asked them: "What does this teach you about what God is like?" We helped them to plan how they would obey what they had learned. Through that one short meeting, we witnessed the power of God's Spirit to bring God's Word alive to people. The husband turned to his wife and told her: "Whenever we argue together, you're not supposed to go back to your parents' house. God has made us to be a team together, so let's ask him to help us solve our arguments ourselves."

After our discussion, we drove the five hours back to our city. We continued to pray for them, and a few weeks later we rang them to find out how they were getting on. To our surprise, they shared with us that they had carried on reading our series of Bible stories. A few evenings earlier, when they reached the end of one of the stories, they had decided to give their lives to Jesus together! They asked if we could drive the five hours back to their village so that we could teach them how to share the stories with their parents and their brothers. After making the ten-hour round trip to help them start their new Discovery Group, Hussein left them to carry on as the group leaders. We still ring them to coach them, but their group is led by them, and not by us. That's what can happen when we follow the Forgotten Manifesto!

We long to see a disciple-making movement sweep across Iraq, and we are excited by these small beginnings. As we attempt to follow the instructions of Jesus to his seventy-two disciples, we are starting to see a new fruitfulness that goes way beyond any of our wildest dreams.

11

Miraculous acceleration

Luke 10:9

"Heal the sick who are there and tell them, 'The kingdom of God has come near to you.'" (Luke 10:9)

Difficult jobs require power tools. It can take hours to cut through metal bars with a hacksaw, but only a few seconds with an angle grinder. It can take a team of men a month to dig foundations for a building with spades and shovels, but it takes one person in a mechanical digger less than a day. In the same way, Jesus tells us that, if we want to make disciples rapidly, we need to learn to use the power tools that he has given us to do so.

The Forgotten Manifesto of Jesus contains a command for the Seventy-Two to "Heal the sick" as living proof that the good news they are proclaiming from the Scriptures is true. Although they are to go slow to go fast with people, they should expect God to accelerate the process by doing things which prove to people that "The kingdom of God has come near to you." Our experience has been that, when we take people on a journey of discovery, we can expect the Lord to perform seven different types of miracles around us as we share (see Figure 11.1).

First, we find God often gives us **prophetic insight** through his Holy Spirit, so that we know things about people's lives that we could never have known naturally. Jesus modeled this for us during his three years of public ministry, because it is a powerful way of capturing people's attention and of granting them faith to begin a journey of discovery. Jesus stunned Nathanael by revealing that he

Prophetic insight

Healing

Deliverance from demons

Restoration

Provision

Conviction

Dreams and visions

Figure 11.1 The "7 Ms" – seven miraculous accelerants toward faith in God

knew all about what happened to him while he was under a fig tree. He shocked Zacchaeus when he greeted him by name, although the two of them had never met before. He astounded a Samaritan woman by revealing that he knew all about her five divorces and her latest flame.[1]

Jesus trained his followers to make this part of their own ministry by sending them on errands that required them to rely on the prophetic insights that the Holy Spirit gave to him. He told them where to find a tied-up donkey and what words they should use to persuade the donkey's owners to lend it to him for his triumphal entry into Jerusalem. He sent them to look for a man carrying a jar of water on his head and to follow him, because they were to celebrate the Last Supper together in his home. As a result of this training, we discover in the book of Acts that prophetic insight played a vital role in how the early Christians sought out People

---

1 Mark 2:8; Luke 19:5; John 1:42, 1:45–51, 4:16–19.

of Peace and discipled them together.[2] Like those early Christians, we find that God gives us prophetic insight which captures people's attention and persuades them that our stories may contain answers to the struggles they are facing.

Once we have begun to take people on a journey of discovery, we find that God gives us opportunities to pray for them to experience **healing** and **deliverance from demons**. As they open up to us more and more about the struggles they are facing, we find that God also enables us to pray for the miraculous **restoration** of what is broken in their lives, such as their relationships with others, and for miraculous **provision** to meet their urgent needs. When people see God at work in the detail of their lives through these four practical miracles, it helps them to believe that God will also forgive them for their sins and transform their lives, as he promises he will in the Scripture stories they are reading.

The last two miraculous accelerants are things that God alone can do in people's hearts. We pray for deep **conviction** to fall on people as they read the Scriptures with us – a growing conviction of their sin and a growing conviction that the stories we are sharing with them are the living words of God.[3] We also pray for God to grant them supernatural **dreams and visions** to convince them that he is real and that they must surrender their lives to him. When we witness these two miracles taking place in people's hearts, we feel like the Seventy-Two when Jesus sent them out ahead of him "to every town and place where he was about to go." Having shared God's Word with people, we find that Jesus follows up on our words by granting people faith to believe what we have said to them.

In the next chapter, we will give you some real-life examples of how these seven types of miracles can accelerate people's journey of

---

2   Matthew 17:24–27; Mark 11:1–6; Luke 22:8–13; Acts 5:1–11, 8:26–40, 9:10–18, 10:1–48, 14:9–10, 16:6–15. See also 1 Corinthians 14:24–25.

3   2 Kings 22:11; Nehemiah 8:9; Romans 3:19–20; 1 Thessalonians 1:4–5, 2:13.

discovery. But first, here are a few of the important lessons that we have learned about how to use these power tools effectively.

First, Jesus commands us to believe in the reality of these miracles. He doesn't simply command us to pray for people to be healed. He promises that he will actually heal them! This was true for the Twelve on their first mission trip to the towns and villages of Galilee. Jesus "gave them authority to drive out impure spirits and to heal every disease and sickness" (Matthew 10:1, Luke 9:1). He "sent them out to proclaim the kingdom of God and to heal the sick" (Luke 9:2). He commanded them to "Heal the sick, raise the dead, cleanse those who have leprosy, drive out demons" (Matthew 10:8). Because they took Jesus at his word and believed this promise, we are told that they "went from village to village, proclaiming the good news and healing people everywhere" (Luke 9:6). Jesus does not water down this promise when he commissions the Seventy-Two. His instructions are the same: "Heal the sick who are there and tell them, 'The kingdom of God has come near to you.'" We need to believe that Jesus grants to all of his followers the same power tools that marked his own public ministry.

> ## "We need to believe that Jesus grants to all of his followers the same power tools that marked his own public ministry."

Jesus really means it when he tells his followers: "Very truly I tell you, whoever believes in me will do the works I have been doing, and they will do even greater things than these, because I am going to the Father" (John 14:12). Knowing that we may doubt it, Jesus states, "Very truly I tell you." Knowing that we may dismiss it as a promise for the Twelve and the Seventy-Two, but not for ordinary, run-of-the-mill believers such as us, Jesus emphasizes that this is a promise for "whoever believes in me." Knowing that we might seek to dilute it, Jesus insists that all his followers "will do the works I have been doing, and they will do even greater things than these." When Jesus ascended back to heaven, he received authority from his Father to fill his followers with the same Holy Spirit who empowered his own ministry. These miracles are possible for all of us, "because I am going to the Father." Jesus insists that he has done all that is required for him to be able to entrust us with his power tools.[4]

Second, Jesus warns us not to regard miracles as a silver bullet for effective evangelism. They are just one element of his Forgotten Manifesto. They are not given as a substitute for taking people on a journey of discovery. If a person's heart is not open toward God, then witnessing a miracle is unlikely to change that. In Luke 10:13–15, Jesus curses several of the towns and villages of Galilee that witnessed the miracles of the Twelve yet rejected the message they heard. Most of the people in Chorazin, Bethsaida and Capernaum were unwilling to be open about their struggles or to express their hunger for God to help them with their lives. The soil of their hearts was so hard that even mighty miracles could not penetrate it, so now Jesus is sending the Seventy-Two elsewhere.

Miracles are most effective when they are witnessed by a person who is already on a journey of discovery. That's why Jesus tells the Seventy-Two to share the good news with people before they perform miracles for them.[5] They are to enter people's homes with a simple greeting: "Peace to this house." They are to engage them in serious and spiritual discussions over dinner. It is only after this,

---

4 Peter declares this triumphant truth in Acts 2:32–33, 2:38–39. Paul also celebrates it in Ephesians 4:8.

5 This is why Jesus preaches from a boat in Mark 3:9–10. It is so important to Jesus that people hear what he has to say to them before they experience what he can do for them that he fortifies himself behind the moat of Lake Galilee so that he can take the crowds on a journey of discovery before they can touch him and be healed.

once they have found a Person of Peace, that they are to perform miracles as proof that the stories they share with them are true: "The kingdom of God has come near to you." The gospel writers describe miracles as "signs" because they signpost people toward faith in what they hear. They can accelerate the discovery process for people, but they cannot act as a substitute for it. For this reason, miracles seldom trigger disciple-making movements on their own. They simply catalyze movements that have already begun and cause those movements to spread rapidly.

"[Miracles] can accelerate the discovery process for people, but they cannot act as a substitute for it."

Miracles are vital power tools, but they are not silver bullets. They are accelerants. They are God's signposts that what people are discovering in his Word must be true. We are told that "Paul and Barnabas spent considerable time there, speaking boldly for the Lord, who confirmed the message of his grace by enabling them to perform signs and wonders."[6]

Almost all of the People of Peace we have brought to faith in Jesus have opened themselves up to the gospel because of a struggle they are experiencing in their lives. For some it is emotional. For others it is mental or relational. For still others it is physical or spiritual. What everyone has in common, however, is that their struggle is what drives them toward exploring faith in God. We know from our own lives that God tends to use the toughest times to draw us closer to him, so it shouldn't surprise us that he does the same thing with nonbelievers. We must therefore resist the urge to offer people quick fixes for their problems. It may feel compassionate to perform miracles straightaway, but if God is seeking to use people's struggles to draw them to faith in him, we

---

6   Acts 14:3. Mark 16:20 echoes this by describing miracles as "signs following" the sharing of God's Word.

aren't being loving if we seek to take the edge off their struggle too early. We are working against God! That's why, instead of offering people quick advice or a cursory prayer, we invite them to begin a journey of discovery. Their miracle will come at the right time within that process.

"We must resist the urge to offer people quick fixes for their problems."

Remember the order of the "7 Ss." Our *simple* and *serious* and *spiritual* conversations invite people to open up to us about their *struggles*. We then ask them questions to *sift* whether or not they are hungry enough for us to introduce them to our *stories*. It is in the context of those stories that we expect them to have a *supernatural encounter* with God. This is the order Jesus followed to help his two companions on the road to Emmaus, and it ought to be our normal order too.

Of course, there are examples in the gospels and in Acts where people experience miracles early on in their journey of discovery. This is OK! When the Holy Spirit decides to act, that trumps everything. The two big questions that we must ask are simply: "Am I seeking to go faster here than God is?" and "If this person experiences a miracle at this stage, will it make them hungrier for God's Word or less hungry?" We want to learn the lesson that Jesus teaches us in Luke 17:11–19, where only one of the ten lepers he heals returns to listen to his teaching. The rest are so excited to be healed that they rush away to do other things.

Whenever someone opens up to us about a struggle they are facing, it is a holy moment. We want to harness the momentum of their struggle to take them on a journey that will offer them something better than a quick fix – a life-changing relationship with God.

East and West: Supernatural encounters

Iran: Reza's story

I was so depressed that I lived in a room on my own for four years. I only left the room to buy cigarettes and food. One of the best doctors in Iran was tasked with helping me, but none of the pills he gave me seemed to make me any better.

One day, when I went out to buy cigarettes and food, I met a man who asked me why my face looked so sad. After I had shared some of my life story with him, he smiled and asked me: "Is that it? My life is so much worse than yours!" When he told me his own story, I was forced to agree, so I asked him, "How come you are so happy and full of life?" The man smiled again and replied, "Do you really want to know? Then drop by my store sometime tomorrow."

When I visited him the following day, he told me some stories about God. He asked me, "Could this be the difference that you need?" I went home and wrestled hard with what he had said to me. I cried out to God, "If this is real then I need you to prove yourself to me!" My house is very old, and every time you walk across the floor the loose tiles move and make a sound. I was alone in the house, but as I prayed I suddenly heard the sound of the loose tiles moving on my floor. My ears told me that somebody had just walked in front of me, but when I opened my eyes I could see no one. The room was filled with something so thick that I could hardly breathe.

I ran back to my friend's store and told him what had happened. He replied, "This is normal with God. You are going to see much more of this." Then he told me more stories about Jesus and asked me, "Do you want to receive this God that you have just experienced?" I was delighted to say yes. I received Jesus into my heart right there in his store.

Iran: Nafi's story

The hardest thing about being a disciple-maker is that you have to follow the direction of the Holy Spirit. But there is a flip side to this too. I can also say that the easiest thing about being a disciple-maker is that you have to follow the direction of the Holy Spirit!

I believe that God has called me to share the good news of Jesus with shopkeepers. That isn't easy in a city where the penalty for attempting to convert a Muslim to Christ is death, but it is made easier by my knowledge that I can't persuade anyone to follow Jesus by my own charm or cleverness. It is all about finding out what the Holy Spirit is doing and then seeking to join him in his work.

Before I go out into the shops in a new area, I always pray, "God, where do you want me to go to, who do you want me to talk to, what do you want me to say?" Then I stop and listen. I might sense the Holy Spirit telling me to ignore all of the shops on a street except for one. Not every shopkeeper is equally open to God at any one time, but when I obey the Spirit's leading I often find that the shopkeeper says something like, "Who are you? The moment you walked into my shop, the hair on the back of my neck stood on end", or "Wow, I know you! Last night I had a dream in which you came to visit me and told me something which completely changed my life."

After we have chatted together, I then rush home and pray some more. I ask the Lord to ensure that the seed which I have sown through our conversation will take deep root in the shopkeeper's heart and that the devil will not be able to steal it away. As I carry on praying, I seek to hear God telling me the right time to go back to their shop to talk with them further. I often find that when I go back, they have received further supernatural dreams or visions of Jesus.

I expect to have to go slow with most people, but when the Holy Spirit works in somebody's heart like this it tends to catapult them forward much more quickly. It is very risky to share your heart with people in Iran, yet shopkeepers often say to me, "I have no idea why I'm telling you this. I have never told anybody else this." I know that I can't persuade anybody to read Bible stories with me, yet I have lost count of the number of times that a shopkeeper has said to me, "I just sense that what you're saying to me is the answer to my problem."

It's not about my skill as a disciple-maker. It's all about God's leading. My friends and I have made a promise to the Holy Spirit that we will never go ahead of him and we will never go behind him. We will always walk alongside him and move exactly as he moves.

Iran: Omid's story

For every action, there is an equal and opposite reaction. That's Newton's Third Law. But as you're about to see, thankfully, God is not bound by physics.

There was a time in my life when I was enjoying much success with my business. I traded gold and foreign currencies for rich clients, and I was very good at it. My cut of the profits gave me far more than I needed to support my wife and daughter. I was rich and successful – and yet I felt an emptiness inside. I knew deep down that this was spiritual, because my relationship with God was soulless. I longed for something more than ritualistic Islamic prayers, so I tried to talk to God in my own way – and he listened. God put me in the path of a man who quickly became a close friend. He began to share amazing stories with me from the Bible about the power of God. This was a new sensation, a stirring like I'd never felt before. This was my answered prayer. I began to reread the stories on my own, and I could feel that God was slowly transforming me.

I began to share these stories with my wife and daughter. We shared the stories together with our friends. We simply couldn't help sharing our experience of God with others. We were so excited that we were able to talk directly to God anytime we wanted. We were so excited that he listened and that we were now in a real, personal relationship with God.

That was the action. Now came the reaction. I suffered a serious setback in my business. The money markets crashed because of foreign sanctions against Iran. In my attempts to circumvent this, I was cheated out of a large sum of money that belonged to my clients. They were furious and started coming to my house daily to demand their money. Over the next month, I slipped into a deep depression. I stopped talking to God and no longer read the stories that were given to me. I even stopped talking to my friend who gave them to me.

But my friend wouldn't give up on me. He continued to call me to encourage me and, eventually, I began to listen once again. I asked the God of these stories for a miracle to resolve my situation. Shortly afterwards, while rummaging through some old papers, I found a legal document which granted me ownership of a small garden that had belonged to my late grandmother. I expected that it would not sell for much money, but what I had forgotten to factor into my calculations was the God of the stories I was reading from the Bible. Due to its location, the price for which I sold the garden was enough to repay my clients completely. I couldn't believe that in just one day, and with just one piece of paper, God transformed everything and took away all my burdens.

I now know that God is faithful, in the good times and the bad. The devil had a reaction to my pursuit of a relationship with the One True God. An opposite reaction? Definitely. Equal? Never!

Former Soviet Union: Vladimir's story

I had begun reading Bible stories with one particular guy. He told me that he believed what he was reading but God really spoke to me and told me that I needed to wait and keep on praying for him.

Three weeks later, I went to visit him. I asked him how God had revealed himself to him during the three weeks that I had been praying for him. He told me, "One week ago I saw these words in my mind: 'Jesus wants to talk to you.' I tried to erase those words from my mind, and I was shocked that I couldn't. Three days later, I had a dream in which I saw a man in white. I couldn't see his face but he wore bright clothing and he presented me with a box. When I opened it, I saw in the box the book that you and I have been reading together. I opened the book and I started to read more of the stories. Every page I turned shone with the brightest light I ever saw in my life."

My friend was upset that he woke up too early and didn't get to finish reading the book in his dream. He asked me, "What is the connection between my dream and the stories that you have been sharing with me?" I asked him to turn with me to the story of what happened to Jesus when he went up on a high mountain with three of his disciples, when his face and clothes began to shine with intense light. After we read it together, I asked him, "What do you think?" He told me, "Now I understand. God wants me to reflect his light from the book you are sharing with me."

America: Jenny's story

Recently I was at a neighborhood party. There was a family there that we had become close friends with. The wife and daughter had both decided to follow Jesus through one of my Discovery

Groups, although the husband had been resistant to going on the journey with them. She came to me during the party and asked if I ever pray over homes to cleanse them of evil spirits. Then she shared with me about a scary struggle that they were facing as a family. She and her husband and their children had all been hearing strange voices around the home, and she had seen a spirit in the form of a woman following her husband around the house. They had become convinced that these were evil spirits that were haunting their home. They were very frightened and didn't know what to do.

While we were talking, the woman's husband joined the conversation. Instead of being angry with her for sharing with me, he confessed to me that he desperately wanted his family to be free from this torment. He didn't know how to make the voices stop so he could feel at peace again in his own home. He too asked me to come and pray a blessing over their home to cleanse it from evil spirits.

For several years, my friends and I had been praying for him to open up to God, so I was tempted to say yes, but I didn't want to give him easy answers. Instead, I told him, "My husband and I could come to your house and pray over your house like you want us to. However, I have an even better solution for you. I recommend that you, your wife and your children go on a spiritual journey together to gain spiritual authority over your home. If your whole family begins following God together, it will be much more powerful than if I just come over one time and pray over your house."

My friend's husband had not been open to the discovery process previously, but this was a desperate moment for him. He was so scared that he asked me, "Can we start tomorrow?" The following day, my husband and I went over and helped him to lead his wife and children in the Discovery Bible Study process. We gave him the questions to ask and started in Genesis 1, then we sat back and watched as this husband led his family in a Discovery Group discussion.

When we checked back in with him two weeks later, we found that they had kept on reading the stories, studying God's Word together as a family and putting it into practice. The husband told us, "Since we began doing this together as a family, we haven't experienced any more spirits in our home. We haven't heard any more voices. We have so much peace and we aren't afraid anymore."

I learned a lot from what happened here. It is sometimes a bit too easy to pray briefly with a person, but taking them through a process of discovery is much more powerful because it teaches them to walk with God for themselves. Instead of trying to address short-term problems, it makes disciples.

12

Should I stay or should I go?

Luke 10:8–16

> "When you enter a town and are welcomed, eat what is offered to you ... but when you enter a town and are not welcomed, go ..." (Luke 10:8, 10)

You don't have to be a big fan of punk rock to know the famous song by The Clash which asks, "Should I stay or should I go?" We have learned to make it our theme tune as we look for People of Peace and seek to steward disciple-making movements all around the world.

Jesus tells the Seventy-Two that there are times when we need to stay and invest time in making disciples. "When you enter a town and are welcomed, eat what is offered to you." We spread ourselves thinly at first to scour the harvest fields for people who are open about their struggles and seem hungry for change, but as soon as we find such people our emphasis changes. We shift our focus toward discipling the People of Peace we have found. "Do not move around from house to house," Jesus warns us, because making disciples is labor intensive. We can only do it effectively by learning to say no to a lot of other things.

Jesus therefore warns the Seventy-Two that there are times when we need to cut our losses and move on. Most of us find this difficult because it feels uncaring, but Jesus insists on it: "When you enter a town and are not welcomed, go into its streets and say, 'Even the dust of your town we wipe from our feet as a warning to you. Yet be sure of this: The kingdom of God has come near.'"

"Jesus therefore warns the Seventy-Two that there are times when we need to cut our losses and move on."

A bit of context is helpful here. At the start of Luke 9, Jesus sends the Twelve to the towns and villages of Galilee. He teaches them how to look for People of Peace and he commands them: "If people do not welcome you, leave their town and shake the dust off your feet as a testimony against them." Jesus says this even more strongly in Matthew's gospel: "Whatever town or village you enter, search there for *some worthy person* and stay at their house until you leave ... If the home is *deserving*, let your peace rest on it; if it is not, let your peace return to you [my italics]" (Matthew 10:11–13). Since most of the people we meet are not People of Peace (at least not at this stage in their lives), Jesus says we need to learn to move on quickly. Time wasted with the wrong people is time we can't invest in the right people. Jesus therefore states firmly that not all people are equally worthy and not all homes are equally deserving of our time.

That's the context for Luke 10. Jesus is about to leave Galilee in order to shift his attention to the other regions of Israel. He will not return to Galilee until after his resurrection, so he uses the commissioning of the Seventy-Two as an opportunity to name and shame those Galilean towns that have failed to embrace his message. Jesus does this to teach his followers that there are times for us to stay and times for us to go. Jesus models for us that "wiping the dust off our feet" means making it clear to people that they have rejected God's offer of life and that we are moving on to seek out People of Peace elsewhere.[1]

This has been one of the hardest lessons for us to learn as *Sheep Among Wolves*. We don't like giving up on anybody! But because we have learned to take Jesus seriously in this instruction, we are

---

1 Jesus now moves southward through Samaria, Perea and Judea (9:51–53, 13:22). The early Christians follow his example by "wiping the dust off their feet" in Acts 8:18–23, 13:8–12, 13:45–51, 14:4–7, 18:4–8, 28:23–28.

starting to see gospel fruit in some of the toughest places in the world. You may find it helpful to turn at this point in your Bible to Luke 18:18 – 19:10, where Jesus unpacks this important principle for us a little further. He wants to teach us the vital skill of knowing how to spot the difference between a Person of Peace and a Rich Young Ruler.

In Luke 18:18–23, Jesus finds somebody who looks like a Person of Peace. He hails Jesus as a "good teacher" and asks him, "What must I do to inherit eternal life?" But there is a reason why **sift** is the fifth of the "7 Ss." Things are not quite as they appear. Before investing his life in discipling this man, Jesus sense-checks whether he is indeed a Person of Peace. He doesn't want to spend the next few weeks having academic discussions with him about eternal life. He wants to take him on a journey of discovery, so he needs to find out how *open* the man is about his struggles, how *hungry* he is for his life to change and how likely he is to *share* whatever he learns with other people.

Jesus tests the man's hunger by challenging his preconceived ideas about what God is like. "Why do you call me good? No one is good – except God alone." Jesus tests the man's openness about his struggles by quoting some of the Ten Commandments to him. On both counts, the man fails the test. Instead of confessing his sins to Jesus and asking him for help to know God better, the man opts for the safe ground of pretending that he has kept all God's commandments since he was a boy.[2] Clearly, he is neither open nor hungry.

There is no commandment in the Jewish law requiring people to renounce their possessions, yet Jesus orders him to "Sell everything you have and give to the poor." He does this to test how eager the

---

2   In the same way, Jesus sifts Jewish hearts by demanding that they "eat the flesh of the Son of Man" (John 6:53, 6:66–69, 7:43) and pagan hearts by dismissing one of them as a "dog" (Matthew 15:21–28). The early Christians sift their listeners in a similar fashion in Acts 14:22 and 1 Thessalonians 3:4.

man is likely to be to share whatever he learns with others. The man responds with sadness, because he likes the idea – on paper – of becoming a disciple of Jesus, but he clearly isn't sad enough to obey. Jesus has sifted the man's heart successfully. He isn't *open* or *hungry*, nor is he willing to *share*.

In Luke 18:24–34, Jesus uses this encounter to teach his disciples how to spot the difference between a Person of Peace and a Rich Young Ruler. He warns them not to waste their time trying to make disciples of the prosperous and self-satisfied. People of Peace do not need to be the brightest or the best, but they do need to be desperate. If you don't know many people who seem desperate to go on a journey of discovery with you, then keep on looking, because "What is impossible with man is possible with God." In Iran, it is relatively easy to find People of Peace, because an oppressive government and an economic crisis have combined to make most people cry out for help from God. In the affluent West, there are many people like them, but we tend to look for them in the wrong places. In the Parable of the Great Banquet in Luke 14:15–24, Jesus directs us to "Go out quickly into the streets and alleys of the town and bring in the poor, the crippled, the blind and the lame." If we find that, despite our fervent prayers, our affluent friends and neighbors feel little hunger for our message, then we are to redirect our efforts toward the lost, the least and the lonely. If Jesus made most of his disciples among the poor and the marginalized, then it shouldn't surprise us if we find ourselves needing to do the same.[3]

To find a Person of Peace, we need to start conversations with lots and lots of people. In the same way that it takes a hundred million sperm to conceive a single baby, we need to sow God's Word widely in order to see people born again. Imagine that your child is sick and dying, but you have heard that there is a doctor who knows

---

3 This does not mean consigning the rich and affluent to hell. Our experience is that, when the rich witness God transforming the lives of "little people," it provokes them to open up about their own struggles too.

how to heal her. You rush to the hospital and are told that the doctor has gone out for lunch, so you visit all of the local restaurants, asking everyone you meet, "Are you the doctor I am looking for?" If a person says no, you don't sit down to see if you can persuade them to study medicine and learn how to heal your child. You recognize that you have not yet found the person you are looking for, and you move on! That's how it is with looking for People of Peace. We need to initiate lots of conversations with people, like Paul did in Athens, when he spent time conversing "in the marketplace day by day with those who happened to be there."[4]

"To find a Person of Peace, we need to start conversations with lots and lots of people."

In Luke 18:35 – 19:10, Jesus models for us what this looks like in practice in the city of Jericho. First, he meets a blind beggar who is as poor as the Rich Young Ruler is wealthy. The beggar has nothing, so he refuses to listen to his neighbors when they tell him to stop shouting so loudly to Jesus about his struggles. Jesus takes this as a sign that he is *open* and *hungry*. When he heals him, nothing can stop the beggar from *sharing* his praises with his neighbors. The whole of Jericho hears that Jesus has come to set people free.

Next, Jesus meets a tax collector named Zacchaeus. This man is wealthy but dissatisfied. He is so desperate for help from Jesus that, because he is short, he is willing to climb a tree to see Jesus as he passes by – something that it was acceptable for a child to do in first-century Jewish culture, but definitely not for a grown man. When Jesus sees him up a tree, he takes it as a sign that Zacchaeus is *open* about his struggles and *hungry* for his life to change. He tests this by inviting himself into the man's home, just as he told the Twelve and

---

4   Acts 17:17. This also helps us not to try to second-guess the harvest. We would never have imagined that a promiscuous Samaritan woman or a demonized madman were People of Peace in John 4 and Mark 5.

the Seventy-Two to do. When Zacchaeus receives him gladly, it is likely that Jesus reads Exodus 22:1 with him, since the tax collector emerges from his house to *share* with his neighbors that he will pay them back four times what he has stolen from them and will give to the poor half of his remaining possessions that were not dishonestly earned. When Zacchaeus does what the Rich Young Ruler refused to do, Jesus hails him as "a son of Abraham." Although he is wealthy, he is a Person of Peace and not a Rich Young Ruler.

This has been one of the hardest lessons for us to learn. We have often tried too hard to persuade people to read our Bible stories with us, forgetting that unless they are *open* and *hungry*, they will inevitably drop out after the first few stories. We have wasted our time with people who love our one-to-one discussions but who refuse to *share* what they are learning with others. It has taken us years to discover that the devil's mission statement can be found in Acts 4:17 – "To stop this thing from spreading any further among the people." One of the main ways that the devil has distracted us is by sending us people who are fun to be with but who aren't really serious about becoming disciples of Jesus.[5]

We cannot state this strongly enough to you. If somebody is fun to be with but they aren't *open* about their struggles, they are not a Person of Peace; they are a Rich Young Ruler. If somebody is happy to read Bible stories with you but they aren't *hungry* to obey God, they are not a Person of Peace; they are a Rich Young Ruler. If somebody is willing to obey God personally but they are not eager to *share* what they are learning with others, they are not a Person of Peace; they are a Rich Young Ruler. You are just wasting your time.[6]

---

5 This is one of the reasons why we rarely pray for persecution to end. It is harder to discern true People of Peace when following Jesus feels easy. We have learned to view persecution as God's sifting mechanism.

6 This doesn't mean that we give up on our friends and family. We pray this loving "curse" over them: "Lord, please break them in front of us so that they will confess their struggles to us and want to read our stories with us."

"The devil's mission statement can be found in Acts 4:17 – 'To stop this thing from spreading any further among the people.'"

In another account of his encounter with the Rich Young Ruler, we are told that "Jesus looked at him and loved him" (Mark 10:21). So, let's not imagine that moving on is unloving. It is the kindest thing we can do for Rich Young Rulers. We look at them and love them by making it clear to them that their hearts are hard toward God. Our experience has been that, when we stop meeting with people, it often stimulates their hunger. It is almost as if they needed the shock of being told that they were spiritual timewasters.

We try to be as kind as possible about this and to leave the door open for the future. It might be as simple as not chasing a person to meet up with us for the next story. If they start chasing us, we can always lean back in. Alternatively, we might give them the next story to read by themselves to see if they come back to us with their answers to the seven questions. This puts the ball in their court, either to chase us or to let our discussions die. For people who refuse to share with others, we might be more direct: "It's great to spend time chatting together but this process works best as a group. Let's wait to meet again until a group of your friends want to journey with us."[7] The key thing is not to chase people in whose hearts God isn't working. We can only find People of Peace, never manufacture them.

It was because Jesus had the wisdom to move on from the Rich Young Ruler that he had time to disciple the blind beggar and Zacchaeus. That's why he tells us very firmly that there are times for us to stay and times for us to cut our losses and move on.

---

7   We much prefer a Discovery Group to fizzle out by week 4 than go to week 20, then fizzle out. If a group is fruitful, we want to invest in it, but if a group is unfruitful, we want to recognize that as quickly as possible and move on.

America: Jenny's story

Several years ago, my husband and I moved to a new neighborhood. One of the first things that struck us was how few of our new neighbors knew each other. By the time we had lived in our new home for a few weeks, we knew more of them than people who had lived in the area for years.

We asked God as a family to show us how to reach our new neighbors. We decided to knock on people's doors and to invite them to a party in our front yard. This seemed better than a party in our backyard because people would feel more comfortable not having to walk through our house and being able to slip away unnoticed if they wanted to leave. We were amazed at how many of our neighbors came. Over sixty people, and the party lasted into the wee hours of the night. We followed this up with more parties in the months that followed. Our neighborhood slowly began to change, as people started getting to know one another.

At a party of sixty people, most conversations remain simple, so we started asking God to show us which people he wanted us to invest more time in getting to know. We then invited them to dinner or to go on a family outing with us. I then invited the moms to join me for a weekly walk together. My husband and I learned to view what we were doing as a funnel. The crowds at our front-yard parties whittled down into a few families in our home, which in turn became a handful of deep friendships on our walks together. In order to have time for this, we had to change our priorities and to spend less time with Christians. We kept praying all the time: "Lord, please lead us to the people you are preparing and drawing to yourself."

Ours is the type of neighborhood where it's easy to imagine that a disciple-making movement could never happen. But as we focused on loving people, we were astounded by what they told us was taking place behind their perfect-looking front yards and front doors. There was a huge amount of loneliness and isolation. Many of them were struggling in secret with alcohol and opioids. We discovered that everyone in every neighborhood has struggles. It just takes some people a little bit longer, and they require a little bit more loving, before they open up to you about them.

During the past few years, we have learned so much from the mistakes we've made. We have spent a lot of time with people who were fun to be with but who were not open or hungry or willing to share what they learned with others. We have spent far too much time attempting to turn Rich Young Rulers into People of Peace. You have to know when it's time to invest elsewhere.

God has taught me a lot through the Parable of the Different Soils. I have come to see that many of our neighbors are the pathway that the seed fell on and the birds snatched it right away. They are fun to be with, but they just aren't interested when it comes to spiritual things. They quickly change the subject or don't respond to what we say. I have learned to keep on loving them, but not to chase them. If their hearts are not good soil, then I can't push them into something they're not ready for.

Other neighbors are like the rocky soil that the seed fell on. At first, they seem open and excited about reading the Creation to Christ stories. But as time goes on, they begin to show signs that their interest in discovering God's plan for their life is superficial. As soon as life gets stressful, or as soon as I ask tough questions about how consistently they are obeying what God is saying to them and sharing it with others, they start to go cold on me, as if I am asking too much of them. They are happy to keep on meeting up to read the stories, but it becomes clear that it is on their own terms. I have learned over time that the obedience and sharing questions that we ask at the end of our Discovery Group discussions really help us to identify Rich Young Rulers. If a person doesn't obey God or share what he is saying to them with others, then I come alongside them to help them a bit more closely. But if they consistently aren't obeying or sharing, I won't put my head in the sand and try to ignore the problem. I recognize it as a tell-tale sign that this person is not ready, and that I need to continue looking elsewhere for people whose hearts have been prepared by God.

Other neighbors are like the thorny soil that the seed fell on. They get excited when God begins to speak to them through Bible stories, but they are too caught up with other things to follow through on what he says. They may be hospitable and a lot of fun to be with, but they simply don't make God a priority. They have time to go shopping, to redesign their home, to be a taxi driver for their kids and to watch endless TV, but God seems to get very little of their time. Although they like the idea in theory of obeying God and sharing what they learn with others, it just never happens because they are so distracted by the world. The reason why they feel no urge to share what they are learning is that they are not obeying God and so their lives are not being transformed. They don't share with others because they don't see the real value in it. Since they are treating what God says to them personally as a nice-to-have, they feel no urgent need for them to pass it on to others.

I have come to recognize that any neighbor whose heart is like the seed that fell upon the good soil must be a neighbor whose heart has been prepared in advance for me by God. As a gardener, I know that good soil doesn't come about by accident. It has to be prepared and watered and given fertilizer. What is true in our backyards is equally true among our neighbors. Only

God can make a person open to receive his Word. Only God can make a person hungry to obey it. Only God can make a person so excited about what they are discovering that they share it with others. People of Peace are miraculously prepared by God to spread the gospel quickly throughout a family or community.

When Jesus met Matthew and Zacchaeus and the woman at the well, the Holy Spirit had already prepared their hearts to receive his message. That's why they immediately followed him and shared what they learned with their neighbors and friends. When Peter met Cornelius, and when Paul met the Philippian jailer and Lydia, the Holy Spirit had prepared their hearts too. Their whole social networks came to faith in Jesus and were baptized with them, and that's what we are looking for too – People of Peace who have been prepared for us by God, not Rich Young Rulers whom we hope we might be able to lead to faith in Jesus on our own.

Every good gardener knows that growing seed takes time, so we need to be gracious and patient with people. We can't expect instant obedience or instant success at sharing the good news with others, but we do want to see daily steps toward obedience and daily attempts to share. One of the most fruitful Discovery Groups that I have started with my neighbors began with a woman who didn't look like a Person of Peace at all. I continued to love her but I didn't invest much time with her. Then suddenly something changed in her life and she came looking for me!

A mentor of mine asks: "How do you find a needle in a haystack? With a really powerful magnet!" As we live visibly spiritual lives that honor God by loving him, by obeying him and by consistently loving our neighbors, we can trust God to work in people's hearts and to attract them to us when they are truly ready for us to disciple them on a journey of discovery.

13

Keep the big picture

Luke 10:17–20

"I saw Satan fall like lightning from heaven ... Rejoice that your names are written in heaven." (Luke 10:18, 20)

Jesus is the ultimate big-picture leader. We are told in Hebrews 12:2 that "For the joy set before him he endured the cross, scorning its shame." He never forgot that he was engaged in a great war with the devil – making disciples, who make disciples, who make disciples.

Luke 10:1–16 is what we would call *training*. Before sending the Seventy-Two out on their mission, Jesus teaches them how to complete it successfully.

Luke 10:17–20 is what we would call *coaching*. It takes place after the Seventy-Two return from their mission, as Jesus follows up his initial training with some on-the-job coaching. His main piece of feedback is that the Seventy-Two must not allow their own skirmishes on the battlefield to distract them from the big picture of their mission. Yes, it is wonderful that Jesus has pledged to use his ordinary followers to bring nonbelievers to faith in him. Yes, it is amazing that he has granted them authority to cast out demons and to heal those who are ill. Yes, it is exciting that they are learning how to foster movements of disciple-makers. But far more wonderful than this is the big picture of God's plan of salvation. Before the world was created, God wrote their names in the Lamb's Book of Life, and when Jesus comes back they will be with God forever.[1] In the meantime, there are many people whose names are in the Book of Life who haven't yet been reached with the gospel. They mustn't allow the joy of their successful skirmishes to distract them from winning this wider war.

Jesus makes this point by reminding the Seventy-Two of the start and finish of the spiritual war in which they are engaged. "I saw Satan fall like lightning from heaven" is a reminder that the war began before the dawn of time. The devil was a beautiful angel who rebelled against God's rule and was expelled from heaven. He knows his time on earth is short before his descent continues down to hell, so he is working hard to take as many humans down with him as possible.[2] "Rejoice that your names are written in heaven" is a reminder that the war will end when Jesus returns in glory to remake the heavens and the earth as his forever home with those who love him and obey him. Disciple-making movements are therefore about something far bigger than the highs and lows of our personal ministry. Each of our own battles is a tiny skirmish in the great, celestial battle that dominates the whole of human history.

Jesus never forgot this during his public ministry. He won the victory for us at Calvary, but he never lost sight of the nations and generations that would be reached with the gospel after he ascended back to heaven. He therefore founded the Church as his leadership development community. He poured out his life to raise up twelve disciples who would go in pairs to seek out People of Peace in the towns and villages of Galilee. He taught each of those pairs how to raise up twelve others to reach the towns and villages of Israel. Those seventy-two would help disciple the 3,000 new believers who received the gospel on the Day of Pentecost. Those 3,000 in

---

1   Jesus is referring here to the heavenly record of the names of all those who are saved. It is mentioned in Exodus 32:32–33; Psalm 69:28; Daniel 12:1; Philippians 4:3; Revelation 3:5, 13:8, 17:8, 20:12, 20:15, 21:27.

2   Isaiah 14:12–15; Revelation 12:7–12. Jesus uses a Greek perfect tense in Luke 10:19 to convey that he has given his people lasting authority and power to defeat Satan and his demons in every generation.

Jerusalem would, in turn, make many more disciples and plant new churches in many other towns and cities.

The good news of the gospel spread very rapidly in the first 200 years of church history because the early Christians held onto this big picture. The apostle Paul urged his disciples to "Follow my example, as I follow the example of Christ."[3] He taught Timothy that this principle must lie at the heart of Christian ministry. "The things you have heard me say in the presence of many witnesses entrust to reliable people who will also be qualified to teach others."[4] That's four distinct generations of leaders in a single verse of Scripture! Paul trained up Timothy, who trained up "reliable people," who trained up many others. Is it any wonder that the early church was such an unstoppable disciple-making movement?

Fast-forward 2,000 years and it's obvious that things have changed. We hear a lot more talk about denominations and about different brands of church than we do about disciple-making movements. Might we be making the same mistake as the Seventy-Two when they came back from their mission? Have we become so caught up in our own local skirmishes that we have forgotten the big picture of the war that we are fighting? There are new nations and new generations that can only be reached through new leaders, so our big need is to raise up and release people quickly to go and make even more disciples.

> **"Have we become so caught up in our own local skirmishes that we have forgotten the big picture of the war that we are fighting?"**

One of the biggest myths about disciple-making movements is that they make disciple-making quicker. That isn't true. They simply

---

3   They were first and foremost disciples of Jesus, but the Greek text of Acts 9:25 also describes them as Paul's disciples. Each of us is to be both a learner and a gatherer of learners. To be a Christian is to be a disciple-maker.

4   1 Corinthians 11:1; 2 Timothy 2:2.

train and mobilize a far larger team of believers, which means that many more disciples are made by the team as a whole. We find it helpful to use the acronym MAWL to summarize how Jesus raised up leaders (see Figure 13.1). He Modeled for people what disciple-making looks like. He Assisted their attempts to make disciples like themselves. He Watched them as they led so that he could give them on-the-job correction. Then he Left to give them space to lead without him. Ascending to heaven, Jesus filled his followers with his Spirit so that they could complete what he had started.

As *Sheep Among Wolves*, this is how we are to make disciples. We seek to **model**, to **assist**, to **watch** and then to **leave**. This is easier said than done. Very few of us believe in people as much as Jesus did when he delegated his authority to the ragtag bunch of disciples who had abandoned him on the night of his arrest and crucifixion. Few of us have the humility that motivated Jesus to tell his followers, "Whoever believes in me will do the works I have been doing, and they will do even greater things than these, because I am going to the Father."[5] To help us to put flesh on the bones of what MAWL looks like in practice, we pursue a model for multiplying our own ministry which you will hear us referring to as "1–4–7–10."

Disciple-making movements are all about releasing People of Peace to lead others on a journey of discovery toward Jesus. Ninety-nine percent of our Discovery Bible Studies start out as a one-on-one discussion, but we can't afford to let them stay that way for long. There is a whole world to be harvested before Jesus comes back from heaven. Since we know that 1+1+1 can never lead to multiplication, we focus from day one on helping our People of Peace to invite their family, friends and neighbors to read the Creation to Christ stories with them. Remember that our

---

5   The promise of Jesus in John 14:12 is not just that we can perform miracles (which would be *the same* works as Jesus). It is that each of us can see disciple-making movements greater in size than his own.

MAWL means that we seek to:

MODEL

ASSIST

WATCH

LEAVE

STORIES 1–2–3
You + Person of Peace (or group)

STORIES 4–5–6
You + Person of Peace + group

STORIES 7–8–9
You remain but Person of Peace is facilitating

STORY 10
You out of the group and background coaching.
Person of Peace is the group facilitator.

Figure 13.1 **MAWL and 1–4–7–10 – how to raise up leaders rapidly**

definition of a Person of Peace is "A nonbeliever who is willing to gather a group of nonbelievers to go on a journey of discovery with them."

The principle of "1–4–7–10" means that we expect to read the first Creation to Christ story with the Person of Peace on their own. Most people want to try out something first before they recommend it to others, and that's OK, but we try to make it clear from the outset that our goal is to help them to gather a group of people in their home to journey with them. The fourth and seventh questions form important bookends to our discussions, because they encourage the Person of Peace to share what they are learning and experiencing with others. We teach them the "7 Ss" so that they don't scare people off by saying too much too early, then we send them out to talk with others.[6] Whatever we fail to emphasize fails to get done, so we focus on helping them to ask the people around them about their struggles.

By story four, we expect a group of people to have started to gather around our Person of Peace. It may just be a couple of other nonbelievers, or it may be as many as ten. What matters is that the Person of Peace has started sharing what they are learning and experiencing with others. This indicates that our work of disciple-making has started spreading through them. For three more weeks, we model how to facilitate an effective group discussion, then we empower the Person of Peace to facilitate by story seven. Since we always ask the same seven questions that allow God's Spirit to speak to people through God's Word, we feel confident that they can facilitate as effectively as we can. Since they are merely the facilitator of their group, and the Holy Spirit is the teacher, they don't need to be special. This is God's disciple-making movement. It isn't ours or theirs.

6 If you need a reminder of the "7 Qs" that we use in all of our discussions, see Appendix, page 189.

"They don't need to be special. This is God's disciple-making movement. It isn't ours or theirs."

We have *modeled* a group discussion and have invited our People of Peace to *assist* us by inviting their friends to join them on the journey. We have taken time to *watch* them as they facilitate the group discussion instead of us, and to give them plenty of on-the-job coaching. By story ten, we therefore feel ready to *leave* the group altogether. We continue meeting up with the Person of Peace to coach them in the background, asking them to give us a synopsis of their last discussion and reading the next Bible story to help them prepare for their next discussion. We may end up spending more time with the Person of Peace at this stage than we did when we were part of their group, but our focus changes. We are now coaching them to be the group facilitator, instead of facilitating ourselves.

This is why we have developed simple disciple-making tools, such as the "7 Es," the "7 Ss," the "7 Qs," the "7 Ms" and the twenty-seven Creation to Christ stories. Everything has to be simple enough for our People of Peace to learn and copy straightaway. Our motto is KISSED – K*eep* I*t* S*hort,* S*imple* and E*asily* D*uplicated* – which is one of the reasons why the gospel can spread so quickly through us. After week four we discourage people from inviting friends into their existing Discovery Groups and encourage them to start new Discovery Groups instead. Our focus shifts toward multiplying groups, rather than merely adding people.

When we share this "1–4–7–10" principle with Christians, many of them get excited. They begin to catch a vision for how the gospel might spread as rapidly in their own nation as it is doing in Iran and in many other parts of the world. However, others get agitated. They are concerned that by allowing nonbelievers to lead Discovery Bible Studies we might propagate heresy. We understand this concern, but we have to say it definitely isn't our experience. Most of the heresies in church history have been started by theologians and learned teachers. We can tell that from the fact that most heresies are named after one of them! Training people to learn directly from the Scriptures is actually a massive safeguard against heresy, since it stops them from relying too heavily on gifted leaders, and it teaches them to weigh everything they hear against the truth of God's Word. The people in our Discovery Groups learn quickly how to correct one another. We can trust the Holy Spirit to teach truth to people when we have the faith to get out of his way.

The fact is, the people around us are already steeped in false teaching. The world is not a neutral space. It is actively persuading people to believe things that are not true. They don't want to come to church because their culture has told them that Christians are peddling a product to them. They don't want to be "told" what to believe. Offering to help them to go on a journey of discovery together, on the other hand, feels hugely attractive. We have to trust that Jesus knows what he is doing when he sends us out into the harvest fields to mentor people in how to hear God's Spirit talking to them through God's Word.

"The world is not a neutral space. It is actively persuading people to believe things that are not true."

Jesus stayed in Sychar for two days to begin discipling the Samaritan woman and her neighbors. Let me ask you a question: Who do you imagine discipled them after day two? The Twelve and the Seventy-Two spent only a few days in the houses of the People of Peace they met in Galilee and the rest of Israel. Peter was only briefly at the house of Cornelius. Paul was forced to flee the homes of Lydia and the Philippian jailer. So, who do you think discipled those people after the apostles moved on? We are given the answer to that question in Acts 14:23. The apostles appointed leaders from within each group and, "with prayer and fasting, committed them to the Lord, in whom they had put their trust."

The willingness of the early Christians to entrust leadership this quickly to people is both shocking and perfectly natural. When a mother duck waddles along the riverbank, the first duckling is following the mother, but every other duckling is following another duckling that is two or three paces ahead of them. The same thing happens in disciple-making movements. The first four elements of the "7 Es" are all about what *we* must do as followers of Jesus to identify People of Peace. The final three elements are all about what we must do to help *them* to form Discovery Groups that become Multiplying House Churches, and that send workers to new sectors of the harvest fields without us (see Figure 13.2).

So keep the big picture. Never forget that Jesus has called us to make disciples, who make disciples, who make disciples. Our local skirmishes form part of a much wider war, through which the Lord Jesus is gathering in God's people right across the world.

Element #1
Be a real disciple to make disciples

Element #2
Pray and mobilize prayer

Element #3
Engage tribes of lost people

Element #4
Find the People of Peace

Element #5
Help them to start Discovery Groups

Element #6
Help them to transition into Multiplying House Churches

Element #7
Coach emerging leaders to go and reach further

Figure 13.2 The "7 Es" – seven essential elements for disciple-making

The fire goes global: Mike's story

Before I became the CEO of Global Catalytic Ministries, I worked for the city of Miami's Fire Department. I feel like my job description didn't change much when I started leading the charity which helps coordinate the disciple-making movement that Jesus started in Iran. Leading our team of disciple-makers around the world means serving the Lord as a spiritual firefighter.

Much of my time is spent fighting spiritual fires started by Satan. There is a reason why Jesus ends his Forgotten Manifesto by promising his followers that he has given them authority to trample on the devil and his demons. I have never experienced such intense spiritual warfare as I have in the past few years. Whether it is a former drug dealer in the Middle East or a homeschool mom in California, all of our team members have discovered that the battle we are fighting together is real.

Praise God, there is also a second type of fire that keeps me busy. The fire of the disciple-making movement that the Lord started in Iran has now spread to seventy-one countries around the world. In 2019, I helped to create a two-hour documentary entitled *Sheep Among Wolves: Volume II*, which told the story of God's work among our group of Iranian underground believers. At the time, our biggest hope was that the documentary might encourage a few Westerners, but God did something far more significant than any of us dreamed. With over five thousand watch parties on launch day worldwide, the documentary went viral on YouTube. It recorded over a million views in its first year! This makes it one of the most watched Christian documentaries of all time. The fire that God had lit in Iran suddenly started spreading.

The fire quickly spread across the border into Afghanistan, although the way this started was very tragic. A group of Western missionaries invited some of the Iranian leaders to come to Kabul in order to share their insights into the Forgotten Manifesto of Jesus. Khadija, who shared her story in an earlier chapter of this book, was there with them, but not everyone was as receptive toward their message as she was. One of the most vocal critics of their teaching from Luke 10 was a Western missionary, who accused them of being afraid to speak the name of Jesus publicly. He rejected the idea of going slow to go fast with people, insisting that he would keep on going out into the bazaars of Kabul and preaching loudly to people in the name of Jesus.

The Iranians pleaded with him to listen. They warned him that this was not their own idea, but the teaching of Jesus, and that ignoring it was likely to get some of the missionaries killed. Tragically, just two weeks after the Iranians returned home to Tehran, we heard on the news that the Western missionary had been murdered by the Taliban, along with his teenage son and daughter.

God used that tragic moment to open the eyes of those Afghan leaders to the Forgotten Manifesto. Even when their nation fell back under the control of the Taliban in August 2021, during the twelve months that followed their house-church network saw many Afghans come to faith in Jesus. This took place under the noses of the strictest Islamic regime in the world. This divine fire is unstoppable!

More recently, we have begun to partner with local believers to start further disciple-making movements in Iraq, in Turkey, in Saudi Arabia, in the Gulf states, in Pakistan and in several other parts of the so-called Islamic world. The apostle Paul celebrates in Colossians 1:6 that "the gospel is bearing fruit and growing throughout the whole world." This is certainly our own experience too.

Then, at the start of 2020, just as our documentary was going viral, the COVID-19 pandemic suddenly shut down the world.

Western Christians were no longer permitted to gather for public worship services in their buildings, and many took it as a once-in-a-lifetime opportunity to reflect on how effectively they were succeeding in the Great Commission. During the long months of lockdown, they arrived at a horrible conclusion. Most of their church growth was coming by attracting existing believers to leave another church and join theirs. Their surveys revealed that the Western church wasn't growing much at all. Teenagers and young adults were leaving in droves. For many Western Christians and church leaders, COVID-19 was a massive wake-up call.

Since their church life had moved onto Zoom, many of these Christians began to reach out to us for answers. The documentary had inspired them, and they wanted to meet with us to process what they felt God was trying to say to them through the COVID lockdown. When they heard some of our insights into the Forgotten Manifesto of Jesus in Luke 10, they got excited. They felt that this was Jesus' answer to many of the questions they were asking. By the end of the pandemic, our influence was no longer confined to Iran and the Middle East. We found that God was calling us to help Christians in North America and Europe to foster disciple-making movements in their nations too. Even now, the Lord is beginning to release his people in the West to break through their traditional structures of containment and control, in order to unleash the wildfire of the gospel.

You have heard a lot about the Iranian Christians and the wonderful things that they have taught us about posturing ourselves like sheep among wolves. I want to be honest with you, however, that there have been tough spiritual fires for us to fight in Iran too. We have found wolves among the sheep, even within the persecuted church. Early in 2023, the board of Global Catalytic Ministries was forced to fire the husband

and wife who were leading our work in Iran. This was due to moral failure, and the board's decision was vindicated by the way that the husband and wife responded with threats to sue us and to endanger the lives of our underground leaders by posting their names publicly. Faced with this legal threat, we were advised not to make any public statement at the time. Instead, we shared the news personally with hundreds of our donors, with our auditors and with the IRS. We also shared it with the president of Ministry Watch, an organization that seeks to ensure the integrity of Christian charities around the world. Now that more than a year has passed, I feel I can at last share publicly about this fire we needed to fight within the Iranian church, even as the wildfire of the gospel spread from Iran to the nations of the world.

You may wonder why I am sharing this with you. Isn't there a danger that it might detract from the message of this book, draining your desire to follow the Forgotten Manifesto of Jesus? I really don't think so. I am being honest with you about this because I want to illustrate that the Iranians are flesh and blood, like you and me. They aren't the heroes of this *Sheep Among Wolves* story. Jesus is. This book is about what Jesus is able to do through anybody, anywhere, who is willing to follow the instructions that he gives us for his Great Commission in Luke 10.

We are living through a moment in church history where scandal after scandal seems to be breaking out across the body of Christ. Especially in the West, leaders are being accused of sexual sin or of bullying or of financial dishonesty. I believe that one of the reasons why this is happening is that we have looked to men and women as our leaders in a manner that borders on idolatry. We need to repent of having looked to our church leaders to feed us, to tell us what we should believe, to parent our kids and to allow us to treat our church community as a safe refuge from the world. We have sinned by abdicating our authority and calling to our church leaders in the same way that the Israelites sinned when they pleaded with Moses to go up Mount Sinai and speak to God instead of them. We have placed a burden on the shoulders of our leaders that God never called them to carry. No wonder so many of them slip and fall under it. This is not how Jesus wants his Church to be!

As a former firefighter, I feel like I can smell the purifying flames of God at work among us at this time. He is determined to purify his Church and to make her an unblemished Bride for his Son. Important as it is for us to learn from Jesus how to multiply disciples, unless we get our hearts right toward God we will end up multiplying unhealthy disciples and chaos in the Church. The apostle Paul speaks into this in Ephesians 5:11–13, when he warns us to "Have nothing to do with the fruitless deeds of darkness, but rather expose them. It is shameful even to mention what the disobedient do in secret. But everything exposed by the light becomes visible – and everything that is illuminated becomes a light."

As we have faced up to this sin within the persecuted Iranian church, we have discovered that the fire of the gospel is strong enough to overcome the devil's work of arson. As we took time out to pray and fast and repent together as a Global Catalytic Ministries team around the world, we found ourselves telling God that we were not following the Forgotten Manifesto because it had borne fruit for our friends in Iran. We were following it because we trust and love Jesus, so we wanted to obey the instructions he had given us! We were not seeking to re-apply a methodology that had worked in other countries. We were seeking to obey the living words of Jesus for his followers in any country!

As we recommitted ourselves to this, we began to see the wildfire of the gospel spread to many new countries. Our disciple-making movement is now reaching forty-six nations across the world, and that number keeps on increasing. As Global Catalytic Ministries, we offer two types of help to people who are interested in rediscovering the Forgotten Manifesto of Jesus. First, we invite them to take part in an online training course, in which we teach them the basic principles of Luke 10:1–24. Next, we invite them to become part of an ongoing online coaching community, where they can find longer-term friendships and mentoring for their day-to-day obedience to the words of Jesus. We offer all of this training and coaching for free, as our gift to the body of Christ. We have received freely, so we freely give away to others. And as we do so, the disciple-making movement that the Lord began in Iran continues to spread like wildfire to many different nations of the world.

We hope that this book has helped you. Even by reading it, you have become part of our amazing *Sheep Among Wolves* story. If you would like to connect with us for the sake of friendship, or to receive some training and ongoing coaching, then we would love to hear from you. Feel free to reach out to me or to one of our other leaders by emailing us at **manifesto@catalyticministries.com**.

14

Blessed eyes to see

Luke 10:21–24

> "I praise you, Father, Lord of heaven and earth, because you have hidden these things from the wise and learned, and revealed them to little children." (Luke 10:21)

Jesus has reached the end of his Forgotten Manifesto. In its final four verses, he does what we seek to do through the sixth and seventh questions in our Discovery Groups. He urges us not just to listen to his Word, but to obey it and to share it with the world.

In verse 21, Jesus makes no attempt to hide his happiness. Do the Seventy-Two grasp the full implications of what he has been teaching them about disciple-making movements? Asking God to lead us to People of Peace in the harvest fields is more than just his *will*. The Greek word *eudokia* at the end of this verse describes it as God's *delight* or *pleasure*.[1] We catch a sense of this when the Holy Spirit fills Jesus with joy over his Father's plan to reach the world. This joyful interaction of the Trinity is meant to remind us that the Forgotten Manifesto of Jesus is magnificent news. It is OK for us to get excited about it! It is so radically different from our own thinking that the proud are bound to miss it. We can only grasp it by divine revelation, and God has chosen to reveal these things to

---

1   "Yes, Father, for this is what you were pleased to do" is better translated "Yes, Father, for this is your good pleasure." So be encouraged. God derives great pleasure from revealing truth to "little people" like you and me.

"little children" – to people humble enough to accept whatever their Father has planned for them.

Jesus is inviting us to join him in this happy dance among the Trinity. Although he could command his angels to complete his Great Commission in a moment, he has chosen to accomplish it through us, so that, through it, we can develop a great relationship with him. If we get excited about disciple-making movements as a missional methodology, but not as a way of deepening our friendship with Jesus, then we are missing the big picture, just as the Seventy-Two were in danger of missing it in verse 17. In all of our training courses, we feel a constant need to emphasize that the Forgotten Manifesto is not a magic recipe for us to follow. It is a glorious invitation from Jesus for us to develop a deep friendship with him by learning to partner with him in his harvest fields.[2]

> **"The Forgotten Manifesto is not a magic recipe for us to follow. It is a glorious invitation from Jesus for us to develop a deep friendship with him by learning to partner with him in his harvest fields."**

In verse 22, Jesus repeats that the Great Commission is all about divine revelation. We cannot manufacture People of Peace for ourselves. We can only discover them by asking God to show us which people's hearts he has prepared to receive our message. Unless God does a deep work in people, few of them are willing to be *open* with us about their struggles. Even fewer of them feel *hungry* for the answers that God's Word can give them, or eager to

---

2 This may be why the Forgotten Manifesto of Jesus leads immediately into a call for us to love the lost, the least and the lonely (Luke 10:25–37) and to sit at Jesus' feet in intimate friendship with him (Luke 10:38–42). Disciple-making movements are not your ticket to church growth and to Christian stardom. They are a call for you to know Jesus deeply, and to show your love by becoming his incarnate presence amid the lost world.

share what they are learning with others. These three vital aspects of a Person of Peace are really signs to us that God has prepared people's hearts ahead of us. The Forgotten Manifesto is therefore far more than a methodology for ministry. It is a way of working with God to bring revelation to people through his Word and by his Holy Spirit.

Our Christian friends need divine revelation too. We are wasting our time if we think we can convince them to regard Luke 10:1–24 as the Forgotten Manifesto of Jesus through our own powers of persuasion. We shouldn't be surprised that some of them feel defensive toward us and ask us the same questions that the Pharisees asked Jesus and his early followers: "By what authority are you doing these things?" "Who gave you this authority?" "How dare you lecture us!"[3] Obedience to Jesus always takes us out of the mainstream, so if Jesus has used this book to stir your heart to follow his Forgotten Manifesto, don't wait to convince the believers around you before you get started. Begin to put the words of Luke into practice, trusting that your fruitfulness will convince them over time.[4]

In verses 23–24, Jesus takes the Seventy-Two aside to a private place so that they can rejoice over his Father's plan with him. He tells them, "Blessed are the eyes that see what you see. For I tell you that many prophets and kings wanted to see what you see but did not see it, and to hear what you hear but did not hear it." Jesus wants them to grasp that God has used their little mission trip to grant them revelation into how his followers are going to succeed in proclaiming the good news of his kingdom to people in every corner of the earth. Prophets such as Isaiah predicted the coming of God's global kingdom. Kings such as David wrote

---

3 Matthew 21:23; John 9:34. When Martin Luther was asked these questions during the Protestant Reformation, he reflected that "Nowhere is true Christianity in greater danger than among those who call themselves reverends."

4 This is what Jesus means in Luke 7:35. Your fruitfulness convinces people better than your arguments.

psalms to celebrate the future coming of that kingdom. But the Seventy-Two have actually witnessed God's promised kingdom breaking through. God has given them "blessed eyes to see." He has granted them insights beyond the reach of those prophets and kings. The big question is therefore: What are you going to do with the insights you have seen?

> **"The big question is therefore: What are you going to do with the insights you have seen?"**

Our *Sheep Among Wolves* story did not begin with a group of clever people stumbling across an effective method for evangelizing their nation. The reason it has spread to many other nations is not because they are persuasive communicators. All of this has happened because God has given people "blessed eyes to see" the Forgotten Manifesto of Jesus.

So let me ask you personally: What are you going to do with what God has revealed to you through Luke 10:1–24? How desperate do you feel to see a disciple-making movement spread rapidly across your nation? How much would you be willing to sacrifice to see that happen? What are you going to do with the "blessed eyes to see" that God has given you to know how you are able to reach your nation with the good news of the gospel?

As you reflect on these important questions, know that Jesus is rejoicing over you as he rejoiced over the Seventy-Two. He wants to come alongside you as you finish this book and to help you form a concrete action plan of how you will obey what he has taught you. Jesus wants to take you aside, as he took aside the Seventy-Two, and to help you to articulate your personal response to what he has taught you through Luke 10:1–24.

He longs to hear you tell him that you are ready to do whatever it takes, and to sacrifice whatever it requires, to devote yourself to following the Forgotten Manifesto of Jesus.

England: Phil's story

Deep down, I knew something was wrong. I just didn't know how to articulate the problem.

Everyone around me thought that I was a successful church leader. Our church had quadrupled in size to over a thousand attenders. The Sunday morning service had multiplied into nine or more such services in several different boroughs of London. People were coming to our church to learn the secrets of our success, but increasingly I felt I had nothing to say to them. Why would anybody want to copy us? What we were doing was exhausting and unsustainable. It was puffing up our egos and creating friction between us. It was causing us to fall out with one another.

When COVID hit, I treated the pandemic as an opportunity to reflect a bit more deeply on these disconcerting feelings. It may sound like I am stating the obvious, but when you are a church leader Sunday comes around every week. There is never space in your diary to step away from the treadmill of ministry to ask whether or not you are actually doing what Jesus told you to do. I took this time out as a chance to work out how much money we were spending as a church for each person we saw saved and baptized. It was colossal! Most of our growth had come through Christians leaving other churches and joining ours, and lockdown was a real eye-opener as to how effectively we were discipling them. Some were drifting from their faith: it was as if they didn't know how to follow Jesus without the props and programs we provided for them. Others felt exhilarated to have so much more free time and reported back that they were enjoying a deeper friendship with Jesus than ever before. I couldn't decide which was worse – people who didn't know how to follow Jesus without our programs or people who found that they were able to follow Jesus far better without them!

Like most people during the pandemic, I spent a lot of time on Zoom. It suddenly became as easy to connect with someone on the other side of the world as it was to connect with the person next door. By God's grace, I found myself connecting with a leader in India who had been deeply affected by the movement that David started among the Bhojpuri people there. As he began to introduce me to some of the principles behind disciple-making movements, I was transfixed. I felt God was answering the massive questions I was asking. At the end of the pandemic, I decided to step down from traditional Christian leadership. I didn't think my church was ready to make the change with me. It didn't seem fair, when I was seeking to shift the goalposts on so much of our ministry.

Within a few weeks of attempting to start over, I was close to quitting. I was able to articulate what was wrong with my old model of ministry, but I didn't really understand what Jesus was trying to teach me to do instead. He graciously heard my cries, because at this point I was introduced to one of the Iranian leaders who was featured in the *Sheep Among Wolves* documentary. Although he had only just met me, he felt God telling him that he should mentor me. This was an absolute game-changer for me. Since then, I have come to realize that, without up-front training and ongoing coaching from experienced disciple-makers, most people end up disappointed and frustrated. Jesus sent the Seventy-Two out in pairs for a reason. We need one another.

I never got to know the real names of the underground church leaders who trained me in the Forgotten Manifesto of Jesus. They use burner phones and fake IP addresses to avoid the Iranian secret police, so they were careful not to compromise their true identities, even to me. Yet they met with me for an hour or two every week for a year, patiently training me in the principles of Luke 10:1–24, then helping me to find an ongoing coaching community within their wider family.

Other than the grace of God, their training and coaching is the reason I am still going. I would even go so far as to say that unless a wannabe disciple-maker finds an experienced trainer and a coaching community, they will never go the distance and see a disciple-making movement where they are. There are simply too many pitfalls that can take us out along the way, and it is just too tempting to go back to familiar and more comfortable modes of ministry. If the twelve disciples needed to be mentored for three years before they could become movement leaders, and they had Jesus as their trainer, then we are fooling ourselves if we imagine we can do it any quicker on our own!

I am still learning. It only takes a few minutes for my phone to upgrade its operating system, but it seems to be taking a whole lot longer to upgrade my operating system for ministry. Old habits die hard and there is a lot to learn! What I *can* say is that Jesus is faithful to anyone who has "blessed eyes to see" what he wants to teach them. He has helped me to find People of Peace who would never have come to the traditional church I led, and he has used the Creation to Christ stories to teach them things my sermons never would.

One of the unlikeliest People of Peace God has led me to is a local barman. The first time I met him, he told me that he was gay and that he was struggling because his boyfriend had just kicked him out of their home. Under my old operating system for Christian ministry, I would have taken him to various Bible texts in order to challenge his promiscuous gay lifestyle. But in the new operating system that we are given in the Forgotten Manifesto of Jesus, we are warned to go slow to go fast with people. We are taught to take them on a journey of discovery, casting ourselves in the role of facilitator and allowing the Holy Spirit to assume his proper role as teacher.

A few weeks into our friendship together, I was coaching him in how to gather a group of his friends at the bar to read the Creation to Christ stories with him. I asked him the usual seven questions, including the one about how he felt his life needed to change as a result of the Bible stories we had been reading together. None of the stories had been about gay relationships. I don't think we had even talked about same-sex attraction at all. We had simply opened up God's Word together and I had trusted God's Spirit to be his teacher. Out of the blue, he told me he had reached a firm decision: "Even if it means I have to be single for the rest of my life, I need to be baptized and follow Jesus."

My wife and I discovered another unlikely Person of Peace at the birthday party of one of our neighbors. She was an alcoholic and the party ended badly, with her falling over and experiencing concussion. Our neighbor had to call an ambulance to take her away.

At the start of the evening, however, she had opened up to us about her struggle with alcohol and we had swapped phone numbers. We were able to call her the following day to ask if she was open to going on a journey of discovery with us. After the second or third story, she woke up early one morning with a hangover and went outside to smoke a cigarette in her garden. As she watched the sunrise, she decided to speak to God about what she had been reading about him in the Bible. She asked him to give her a sign that he was real. Suddenly a powerful wind began blowing through her garden. She felt a sudden sense that God was with her and was enveloping her with his arms of love. When we baptized her a few weeks later, she shared the story of her conversion with her friends and family. She is now seeking to share the stories with the other women on her rehab program.

Shifting operating systems isn't easy, but it is worth it! Isn't one of the reasons why you began reading this book that you have a nagging sense that something in your ministry needs to change?

I have authored this book in order to help you to do that. I know how much it is going to cost you, because I have paid that cost myself, but I also know that you will not regret it. I am so grateful to God for ambushing me and for giving me "blessed eyes to see" what he wants to do in our generation.

So, what is your concrete action plan from here? What will you do with the things that Jesus has taught you from Luke 10:1–24?

How are you going to respond to the Forgotten Manifesto of Jesus?

If you would like to connect with us for the sake of friendship or to receive our six-week training and become part of our ongoing coaching, then we would love to hear from you at:
manifesto@catalyticministries.com

You can also begin to partner with us through prayer and finance by visiting:
https://catalyticministries.com/

Appendix
The disciple-maker's toolkit

The three commissions

#1: To the Twelve
Matthew 10:1–42

[1]Jesus called his twelve disciples to him and gave them authority to drive out impure spirits and to heal every disease and sickness. [2]These are the names of the twelve apostles: first, Simon (who is called Peter) and his brother Andrew; James son of Zebedee, and his brother John; [3]Philip and Bartholomew; Thomas and Matthew the tax collector; James son of Alphaeus, and Thaddaeus; [4]Simon the Zealot and Judas Iscariot, who betrayed him. [5]These twelve Jesus sent out with the following instructions: "Do not go among the Gentiles or enter any town of the Samaritans. [6]Go rather to the lost sheep of Israel. [7]As you go, proclaim this message: 'The kingdom of heaven has come near.' [8]Heal the sick, raise the dead, cleanse those who have leprosy, drive out demons. Freely you have received; freely give.

[9]"Do not get any gold or silver or copper to take with you in your belts – [10]no bag for the journey or extra shirt or sandals or a staff, for the worker is worth his keep. [11]Whatever town or village you enter, search there for some worthy person and stay at their house until you leave. [12]As you enter the home, give it your greeting. [13]If the home is deserving, let your peace rest on it; if it is not, let your peace return to you. [14]If anyone will not welcome you or listen to your words, leave that home or town and shake the dust off your feet. [15]Truly I tell you, it will be more bearable for Sodom and Gomorrah on the day of judgment than for that town.

[16]"I am sending you out like sheep among wolves. Therefore be as shrewd as snakes and as innocent as doves. [17]Be on your guard; you will be handed over to the local councils and be flogged in the synagogues. [18]On my account you will be brought before governors and kings as witnesses to them and to the Gentiles. [19]But when they

arrest you, do not worry about what to say or how to say it. At that time you will be given what to say, [20]for it will not be you speaking, but the Spirit of your Father speaking through you.

[21]"Brother will betray brother to death, and a father his child; children will rebel against their parents and have them put to death. [22]You will be hated by everyone because of me, but the one who stands firm to the end will be saved. [23]When you are persecuted in one place, flee to another. Truly I tell you, you will not finish going through the towns of Israel before the Son of Man comes.

[24]"The student is not above the teacher, nor a servant above his master. [25]It is enough for students to be like their teachers, and servants like their masters. If the head of the house has been called Beelzebul, how much more the members of his household!

[26]"So do not be afraid of them, for there is nothing concealed that will not be disclosed, or hidden that will not be made known. [27]What I tell you in the dark, speak in the daylight; what is whispered in your ear, proclaim from the roofs. [28]Do not be afraid of those who kill the body but cannot kill the soul. Rather, be afraid of the One who can destroy both soul and body in hell. [29]Are not two sparrows sold for a penny? Yet not one of them will fall to the ground outside your Father's care. [30]And even the very hairs of your head are all numbered. [31]So don't be afraid; you are worth more than many sparrows.

[32]"Whoever acknowledges me before others, I will also acknowledge before my Father in heaven. [33]But whoever disowns me before others, I will disown before my Father in heaven.

[34]"Do not suppose that I have come to bring peace to the earth. I did not come to bring peace, but a sword. [35]For I have come to turn

"'a man against his father,

a daughter against her mother,

a daughter-in-law against her mother-in-law—

[36] a man's enemies will be the members of his own household.'

[37]"Anyone who loves their father or mother more than me is not worthy of me; anyone who loves their son or daughter more than me is not worthy of me. [38]Whoever does not take up their cross and follow me is not worthy of me. [39]Whoever finds their life will lose it, and whoever loses their life for my sake will find it.

[40]"Anyone who welcomes you welcomes me, and anyone who welcomes me welcomes the one who sent me. [41]Whoever welcomes a prophet as a prophet will receive a prophet's reward, and whoever welcomes a righteous person as a righteous person will receive a righteous person's reward. [42]And if anyone gives even a cup of cold water to one of these little ones who is my disciple, truly I tell you, that person will certainly not lose their reward."

Mark 6:6–13

Then Jesus went around teaching from village to village. [7]Calling the Twelve to him, he began to send them out two by two and gave them authority over impure spirits. [8]These were his instructions: "Take nothing for the journey except a staff – no bread, no bag, no money in your belts. [9]Wear sandals but not an extra shirt. [10]Whenever you enter a house, stay there until you leave that town. [11]And if any place will not welcome you or listen to you, leave that place and shake the dust off your feet as a testimony against them." [12]They went out and preached that people should repent. [13]They drove out many demons and anointed many sick people with oil and healed them.

Luke 9:1–6

[1]When Jesus had called the Twelve together, he gave them power and authority to drive out all demons and to cure diseases, [2]and he sent them out to proclaim the kingdom of God and to heal the sick. [3]He told them: "Take nothing for the journey – no staff, no bag, no bread, no money, no extra shirt. [4]Whatever house you enter, stay there until you leave that town. [5]If people do not welcome you,

leave their town and shake the dust off your feet as a testimony against them." ⁶So they set out and went from village to village, proclaiming the good news and healing people everywhere.

#2: To the Seventy-Two
Luke 10:1–24

¹After this the Lord appointed seventy-two others and sent them two by two ahead of him to every town and place where he was about to go. ²He told them, "The harvest is plentiful, but the workers are few. Ask the Lord of the harvest, therefore, to send out workers into his harvest field. ³Go! I am sending you out like lambs among wolves. ⁴Do not take a purse or bag or sandals; and do not greet anyone on the road.

⁵"When you enter a house, first say, 'Peace to this house.' ⁶If someone who promotes peace is there, your peace will rest on them; if not, it will return to you. ⁷Stay there, eating and drinking whatever they give you, for the worker deserves his wages. Do not move around from house to house.

⁸"When you enter a town and are welcomed, eat what is offered to you. ⁹Heal the sick who are there and tell them, 'The kingdom of God has come near to you.' ¹⁰But when you enter a town and are not welcomed, go into its streets and say, ¹¹"Even the dust of your town we wipe from our feet as a warning to you. Yet be sure of this: The kingdom of God has come near.' ¹²I tell you, it will be more bearable on that day for Sodom than for that town.

¹³"Woe to you, Chorazin! Woe to you, Bethsaida! For if the miracles that were performed in you had been performed in Tyre and Sidon, they would have repented long ago, sitting in sackcloth and ashes. ¹⁴But it will be more bearable for Tyre and Sidon at the judgment than for you. ¹⁵And you, Capernaum, will you be lifted to the heavens? No, you will go down to Hades.

¹⁶"Whoever listens to you listens to me; whoever rejects you rejects me; but whoever rejects me rejects him who sent me."

[17]The seventy-two returned with joy and said, "Lord, even the demons submit to us in your name." [18]He replied, "I saw Satan fall like lightning from heaven. [19]I have given you authority to trample on snakes and scorpions and to overcome all the power of the enemy; nothing will harm you. [20]However, do not rejoice that the spirits submit to you, but rejoice that your names are written in heaven."

[21]At that time Jesus, full of joy through the Holy Spirit, said, "I praise you, Father, Lord of heaven and earth, because you have hidden these things from the wise and learned, and revealed them to little children. Yes, Father, for this is what you were pleased to do.

[22]"All things have been committed to me by my Father. No one knows who the Son is except the Father, and no one knows who the Father is except the Son and those to whom the Son chooses to reveal him."

[23]Then he turned to his disciples and said privately, "Blessed are the eyes that see what you see. [24]For I tell you that many prophets and kings wanted to see what you see but did not see it, and to hear what you hear but did not hear it."

#3: To every follower
Matthew 28:16–20

[16]Then the eleven disciples went to Galilee, to the mountain where Jesus had told them to go. [17]When they saw him, they worshiped him; but some doubted. [18]Then Jesus came to them and said, "All authority in heaven and on earth has been given to me. [19]Therefore go and make disciples of all nations, baptizing them in the name of the Father and of the Son and of the Holy Spirit, [20]and teaching them to obey everything I have commanded you. And surely I am with you always, to the very end of the age."

The "7 Es" – seven essential elements for disciple-making

Element #1
Be a real disciple to make disciples

Element #2
Pray and mobilize prayer

Element #3
Engage tribes of lost people

Element #4
Find the People of Peace

Element #5
Help them to start Discovery Groups

Element #6
Help them to transition into Multiplying House Churches

Element #7
Coach emerging leaders to go and reach further

Figure 2.1

The "7 Ss" – seven stages in a go-slow-to-go-fast gospel conversation

SIMPLE

⌄

SERIOUS

⌄

SPIRITUAL

⌄

STRUGGLE

⌄

SIFT

⌄

STORIES

⌄

SUPERNATURAL ENCOUNTER

Figure 7.1

The "7 Qs" – seven questions to ask in a Discovery Group discussion

1 **What are we thankful for?**
   DNA of Worship

2 **What are we struggling with?**
   DNA of Prayer

3 **How can we help people with their struggles?**
   DNA of Ministry

4 **How did we do with our action steps from last time?**
   DNA of Accountability

   Read / reread / retell the Bible story

5 **What does this teach us about God and about people?**
   DNA of Discovery

6 **What do we feel led to change after reading this story?**
   DNA of Obedience

7 **Who will we share with this week?**
   DNA of Evangelism

Figure 8.1

The "7 Ms" – seven miraculous accelerants toward faith in God

Prophetic insight

Healing

Deliverance from demons

Restoration

Provision

Conviction

Dreams and visions

Figure 11.1

MAWL and 1–4–7–10 – how to raise up leaders rapidly

MAWL means that we seek to:

MODEL

ASSIST

WATCH

LEAVE

STORIES 1–2–3
You + Person of Peace (or group)

STORIES 4–5–6
You + Person of Peace + group

STORIES 7–8–9
You remain but Person of Peace is facilitating

STORY 10
You out of the group and background coaching.
Person of Peace is the group facilitator.

Figure 13.1

Common struggles

Emotional

Anger

Anxiety

Shame / Guilt

Sadness

Divorcing parents

Bereavement

Relational

Conflict

Betrayal

Rejection

Abuse

Marriage issues

Longing for love

Mental

Addiction

Depression

Hopelessness

Suicidal thoughts

Disappointment

Self-loathing

Physical

Overeating

Smoking

Health issues

Disability

Lack of job or career

Poverty

Homelessness

Debt

Trapped in the country

Spiritual

Emptiness

Lack of purpose

Dissatisfaction

Fear

Tormented thoughts

Encountering demons

Trapped by the occult

Worried about eternity

Longing to know God

Figure 7.2

Creation to Christ stories with key truths – 27 key passages with key truths for each

1 **Genesis 1:1 – 2:3** – God creates the world
   Key truth to discover: *There is a God and he created the world. He is very powerful and very good.*

2 **Genesis 2:4–25** – God creates man and woman
   Key truth to discover: *God created man and woman. His plan for them was good and unrestrictive.*

3 **Genesis 3:1–13** – Man and woman disobey God
   Key truth to discover: *People rebel against God's perfect plan. This destroys God's perfect world.*

4 **Genesis 3:14–24** – God judges a sinful world
   Key truth to discover: *God judges humanity, yet he also finds a way to extend mercy.*

5 **Genesis 6:5 – 7:24** – God destroys evil humanity
   Key truth to discover: *There are consequences to human sin, yet God finds a way to extend mercy.*

6 **Genesis 8:1 – 9:17** – God's covenant with Noah
   Key truth to discover: *God resets his creation through judgment in order to maintain new life.*

7 **Genesis 12:1–8, 15:1–6, 17:1–7** – God's covenant with Abraham
   Key truth to discover: *God chooses Abraham to be his friend. To be God's friend is to be blessed by him.*

8 **Genesis 22:1–19** – Abraham gives his son as an offering
   Key truth to discover: *God tests Abraham's faith to deepen their friendship and his blessing.*

9 **Exodus 12:1–28** – The promise of Passover
   Key truth to discover: *God demonstrates his desire and his power to protect his people.*

10 **Exodus 20:1–21** – The Ten Commandments
   Key truth to discover: *God gives his good commandments to his people.*

11 **Leviticus 4:1–35** – The sin offering
   Key truth to discover: *God made a way for sinful people to be forgiven by shedding innocent blood.*

12 **Isaiah 53:1–12** – The promise of a better way
   Key truth to discover: *God provides a better blood sacrifice to forgive his sinful people.*

Figure A.1

13   **Luke 1:26–38, 2:1–20** – The birth of Jesus
    Key truth to discover: *Jesus is born according to the ancient prophecies.*

14   **Matthew 3:1–17; John 1:29–34** – Jesus is baptized
    Key truth to discover: *John testifies that Jesus is the promised Son of God.*

15   **Matthew 4:1–11** – Jesus is tested
    Key truth to discover: *The devil tempts Jesus but Jesus remains the sinless Savior.*

16   **John 3:1–21** – Jesus and Nicodemus
    Key truth to discover: *Jesus is God's only Son, sent to save the world.*

17   **John 4:1–26, 39–42** – Jesus and the woman at the well
    Key truth to discover: *Jesus is the promised Messiah.*

18   **Luke 5:17–26** – Jesus heals the paralyzed man
    Key truth to discover: *Jesus has authority to forgive and to heal.*

19   **Mark 4:35–41** – Jesus calms the storm
    Key truth to discover: *Jesus has authority over the elements of the earth.*

20   **Mark 5:1–20** – Jesus casts out evil spirits
    Key truth to discover: *Jesus has authority over evil spirits.*

21   **John 11:1–44** – Jesus raises a man from the dead
    Key truth to discover: *Jesus has authority over sickness and death.*

22   **Matthew 26:17–30** – Jesus predicts his betrayal and the New Covenant
    Key truth to discover: *Jesus allows Judas to betray him to create a New Covenant between God and man.*

23   **John 18:1 – 19:16** – Jesus is betrayed and condemned
    Key truth to discover: *Jesus is betrayed, falsely accused and numbered among sinners.*

24   **Luke 23:32–56** – Jesus is crucified
    Key truth to discover: *Jesus dies as prophesied, yet as he does so he forgives.*

25   **Luke 24:1–35** – Jesus conquers death
    Key truth to discover: *Jesus is raised back to life as prophesied.*

26   **Luke 24:36–53** – Jesus appears and ascends
    Key truth to discover: *Jesus has returned to heaven. He commissions his followers to proclaim the good news that God forgives anyone who believes in the sacrifice of his Son.*

27   **John 3:1–21** – We have a choice to make
    Key truth to discover: *If we believe in Jesus the Messiah, we will have eternal life.*

Figure A.1 (*continued*)

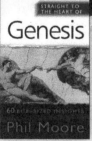

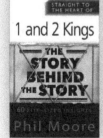

STRAIGHT TO THE HEART SERIES
TITLES AVAILABLE: OLD TESTAMENT

9780857219763

9780857214287

9780857214263

9780857219787

9780857217547

9780857219886

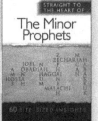

9780857218377

STRAIGHT TO THE HEART SERIES
TITLES AVAILABLE: **NEW TESTAMENT**

9781854249883

9780857216427

9780857217998

9780857212535

9781854249890

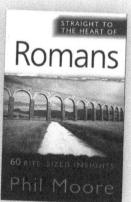

9780857210579